Ben Jonson, Renaissance Dramatist

Ben Jonson,
Renaissance Dramatist

Sean McEvoy

Edinburgh University Press

© Sean McEvoy, 2008

Edinburgh University Press Ltd
22 George Square, Edinburgh

Typeset in 11.5/13 Monotype Ehrhardt
by Servis Filmsetting Ltd, Manchester and
printed and bound in Great Britain by
Antony Rowe Ltd, Chippenham, Wilts

A CIP record for this book is available from the British Library

ISBN 978 0 7486 2301 3 (hardback)
ISBN 978 0 7486 2302 0 (paperback)

Contents

Acknowledgements

I must first thank Joe Moshenska, whose wise and tactful comments on the work in progress have made an invaluable contribution to this book. I would also like to thank Helen Hargest at the Shakespeare Institute for her assistance. Martin Ballard was most helpful with the Chronology. Jackie Jones has been a tactful, encouraging and wonderfully supportive editor. And, of course, the greatest thanks of all go to Nicky and Julia.

List of abbreviations used

Alch.	*The Alchemist*
Conv.	*Conversations with Drummond*
Disc.	*Timber, or Discoveries*
SW	*Epicoene, or the Silent Woman*
Epig.	*Epigrams*
HSS	*Ben Jonson*, ed. C. H. Herford and Percy and Evelyn Simpson, 11 vols (Oxford: Oxford University Press, 1925–52)
Volp.	*Volpone*
Wilkes	*Ben Jonson, The Complete Plays*, ed. G. A. Wilkes, 4 vols (Oxford: Oxford University Press, 1981–2)

Illustrations

Chronology

	Plays and playwrights	Theatre and politics
1564	Shakespeare born Marlowe born	
1570		Queen Elizabeth excommunicated by Pope Pius V
1572	Jonson born	Bartholomew's Eve Massacre in France
1576		James Burbage opens The Theatre
1578	Webster born (?)	
1580	Middleton born	Last performance of miracle plays at Coventry
1587	Kyd *The Spanish Tragedy* Marlowe *Tamburlaine*	Mary Queen of Scots executed. Rose Theatre opens
1588	Marlowe *Dr Faustus*	Defeat of Spanish Armada
1589	Marlowe *The Jew of Malta*	
1592	Marlowe *Edward II* Marlowe *Massacre at Paris* Shakespeare *Richard III*	Azores expedition

	Plays and playwrights	Theatre and politics
1593	Marlowe killed Shakespeare *The Taming of the Shrew*	
1594	Shakespeare *Titus Andronicus*	First of four bad harvests
1595	Shakespeare *Richard II*	Spanish raids on Cornwall. O'Neill's revolt in Ireland
1597	Jonson *The Case is Altered* Shakespeare *The Merchant of Venice*	Private Blackfriars Theatre constructed
1599	Shakespeare *Julius Caesar*	Satires proscribed and burnt. Globe Theatre opens
1600	Marston *Antonio's Revenge* Shakespeare *Hamlet*	Fortune Theatre opens. East India Company founded. Children of the Chapel at the Blackfriars Theatre
1601	Dekker *Satiromastix* Jonson *Poetaster* Shakespeare *Twelfth Night*	Essex's rebellion and execution. Defeat of joint Irish/Spanish army in Ireland
1603	Jonson *Sejanus* Marston *The Malcontent*	Death of Elizabeth; accession of James I. Lord Chamberlain's Men become the King's Men
1604	Chapman *Bussy D'Ambois* Shakespeare *Measure for Measure* Shakespeare *Othello*	
1605	Middleton *A Mad World, My Masters* Shakespeare *King Lear*	Gunpowder Plot

	Plays and playwrights	Theatre and politics
1606	Jonson *Volpone* Middleton *Michaelmas Term* Middleton *The Revenger's Tragedy* Shakespeare *Macbeth*	
1607	Shakespeare *Antony and Cleopatra*	
1608		King's Men lease the Blackfriars Theatre
1610	Beaumont and Fletcher *The Maid's Tragedy* Jonson *The Alchemist*	
1611	Dekker and Middleton *The Roaring Girl* Jonson *Catiline* Shakespeare *The Winter's Tale* Shakespeare *The Tempest*	Authorised Version of the Bible published
1612	Webster *The White Devil*	
1613		Overbury scandal begins. Globe Theatre burns down
1614	Jonson *Bartholomew Fair* Webster *The Duchess of Malfi*	
1615	Middleton and Rowley *A Fair Quarrel*	
1616	Jonson *The Devil is an Ass* Middleton *The Witch* Shakespeare dies	Jonson Folio published
1617	Webster *The Devil's Lawcase*	Jonson made Poet Laureate
1618		Thirty Years War begins

	Plays and playwrights	Theatre and politics
1621	Middleton *Women Beware Women*	
1622	Middleton and Rowley *The Changeling*	
1623		Prince Charles's unsuccesful visit to Spain to marry the Infanta. Shakespeare First Folio published
1624	Middleton *A Game at Chess*	
1625		James I dies; accession of Charles I
1626	Jonson *The Staple of News*	
1627	Middleton dies	Failure of La Rochelle expedition
1628		Petition of Right
1629		Buckingham assassinated. Beginning of Charles I's personal rule
1630?	Ford *'Tis Pity She's a Whore*	
1632	Webster dies (?) Jonson *The Magnetic Lady*	
1637	Jonson dies	

EUP JOURNALS ONLINE
The Ben Jonson Journal

ISSN   1079-3453

eISSN   1755-165X

Two issues per year

The *Ben Jonson Journal* is a twice-a-year review (previously an annual) devoted to the study of Ben Jonson and the culture in which his manifold literary efforts thrived. It aims to contain well written essays on poetry, theatre, criticism, religion, law, the court, the curriculum, medicine, commerce, the city, and family life.

The journal is also concerned with the manifestation of these and other interests in Renaissance life and culture generally and so contains material not only concerning Jonson specifically but of significance to the age in which he lived.

More journals from EUP
African Studies
Historical Studies
Islamic Studies
Linguistics
Literary Studies
Film, Media & Cultural Studies
Philosophy and Religion
Politics and Law
Science and Medical

Edinburgh
University Press

**View full text of all
EUP journals at
www.eupjournals.com**

Introduction

This book is concerned only with Ben Jonson's plays, not his masques, criticism or considerable output of poetry. It makes no sustained attempt to put Jonson's comedies and tragedies in the context of his other writing, but treats them as freestanding works in their own right, as they are experienced in the theatre. Jonson is not in any case a writer with a consistent viewpoint across his *œuvre*.[1] Although all of his work for the theatre is considered, there is a particular focus on what is normally regarded as the middle part of his career, between *Sejanus* (1603) and *The Devil is an Ass* (1616). These are the Jonson texts most frequently studied in further and higher education. They are also, in my opinion, the most innovative, entertaining, profound and brilliant of his plays. I would claim that the comedies, at least, have few rivals in all of English drama.

After an introduction to Ben Jonson and his intellectual and literary inheritance, the following chapters on the plays themselves all take the same format. After a discussion of relevant historical and literary contexts, I offer a commentary on each play. What is distinctive about this book on Jonson is that the principal concern of this section of each chapter is on the audience's experience of the play in performance. Jonson's most distinguished twentieth-century editors were denied the experience of fine production in their day. Otherwise they would never have written in 1925 that his comedies are 'poor in laughter', and the tragedies 'poor in passion and in tears' (HSS II: 127). The theatricality of Jonson's plays is now belatedly recognised as their main virtue; they are to be best appreciated as theatre scripts, not primarily as 'literature'. I hope to do justice to what one director called 'the incredible mixture of animality and intellectuality, of boldness and sharp critical sense' in Jonson's plays (Jensen 1985: 103). As long ago as 1935 R. G. Noyes wrote of *The Alchemist* that 'the play as absolute drama . . . is much more exciting and important than the subject it represents.' The 'absolute drama' of Jonson will be my bias in these parts of each main chapter (Noyes 1935: 104).

The next section of each chapter gives an account of notable recent criticism of each play. The accent here is on work which does regard Jonson's theatre from the literary-critical perspective.

The final section is on the play in performance. I do not offer here a history of the play in the theatre, such as is usually found in introductions to individual editions of the plays. Productions of Jonson have rarely been indifferent. They seem either to succeed brilliantly or to bore utterly. I take the view that these plays are not open texts to be fruitfully interpreted on stage in a thousand different ways. When they work it seems to be because the director and cast have discovered the single right way of performing each individual play within the parameters offered by the sounds, rhythms and structures of Jonson's text. My examination of the plays in performance sets out to identify this 'right way' in accounts of productions from 1660 until 2006. Though Jonson's London is a very distant place from any modern English-speaking city today, there still seems to be a large enough basis of shared language, culture, politics and theatrical convention to make the plays really work. To recycle a very old joke, when rare Ben Jonson is well done he makes the most nourishing theatrical fare. He makes us laugh with delight, and makes us think profoundly about both art and our own lives.

All references to Jonson's plays are from Wilkes. References to other works by Jonson are from Donaldson's edition (Jonson 1985). All references to Shakespeare are from Shakespeare 1997. Spelling and punctuation in quotations from other early modern texts have been modernised throughout.

NOTE

1. See Dutton 1996: 8 and Maus 1984: 48, 182.

CHAPTER I

Life and Culture

JONSON'S LIFE

Ben Jonson was born in June 1572, on the site of what is now Charing Cross station in London. His father died shortly before his birth.[1] His mother remarried a master bricklayer, probably one Robert Brett. Jonson was educated at the nearby Westminster School under the noted humanist scholar and educationalist William Camden. Jonson later paid Camden the compliment of being the man 'to whom I owe/ All that I am in arts, all that I know' (*Epig.*, XIV, 1–2). For some reason his education at Westminster was never completed, and instead of university he was apprenticed to his bricklayer stepfather.

Jonson abandoned this profession to serve for a short time as a soldier in the English army fighting the Spanish in the Netherlands. Here he claimed to have defeated an enemy soldier in single combat, and taken his weapons and armour (*Conv.*, ll. 199–200). Back in England he returned to his 'wonted study' (*Conv.*, l. 201) and married Anne Lewis in 1594. By 1597 he was an actor in the Earl of Pembroke's company and had become a playwright. It appears that he remained part of the Bricklayers' Guild as late as 1611; he was, it seems, to have need of another source of income at times in the troubled few years ahead.

In 1597 Jonson collaborated on a lost comedy, *The Isle of Dogs*, which was condemned by the Queen's Privy Council as 'a lewd play . . . containing very seditious and slanderous matter' (Kay 1995: 18). After two months in prison he began to write for the impresario Philip Henslowe, for whom he produced the play which established him on the London stage, *Every Man In His Humour* (1598). Shortly after the play's first performance, however, Jonson killed the actor Gabriel Spencer in a fight outside a Hoxton tavern. We do not know the origin of the dispute. Spencer had been imprisoned with Jonson for his part in *The Isle of Dogs*. Jonson escaped hanging because he could plead 'benefit of clergy', an archaic privilege from ecclesiastical law which protected the literate from execution at the hands of the crown. All his property was nevertheless confiscated, and he found himself temporarily back in prison for debt in late 1599. Jonson stated that during his time in prison after killing Spencer he converted to Catholicism and remained a Catholic for the next twelve years (*Conv.*, 205–6).

In the final years of Elizabeth's reign Jonson wrote the plays often known as the 'comical satires': *Every Man Out of His Humour* (1599), *Cynthia's Revels* (1600) and *Poetaster* (1601). These last two plays contained barely concealed mockery of the work of two other dramatists, John Marston and Thomas Dekker, who in turn lampooned Jonson in their own plays (see below, pp. 18–19). This so-called 'war of the theatres' was soon over, and Jonson turned to tragedy. We know that he was paid by Henslowe for 'additions' to Kyd's *The Spanish Tragedy* in 1602, and wrote a lost play about Richard III as well as his first Roman tragedy, *Sejanus* (1603).

By this time Jonson was living under the patronage of noblemen, firstly Sir Robert Townshend and then Lord Aubigny. We know he was away from his family when his eldest son Benjamin died in 1603. *Sejanus* once more landed him in trouble with the Privy Council, accused of 'popery and treason' (*Conv.*, 273). Neither this nor his Catholicism prevented him from being commissioned to write for King James I's coronation festivities in 1604, nor from being employed by the Privy Council to give safe conduct to a Catholic priest who was supposed to have evidence about the Gunpowder Plot conspiracy of 1605. The new regime showed favour and he began to prosper. Jonson continued to write masques and entertainment for the court throughout James's life. Even so, Jonson had been imprisoned for the fourth time because of his tactless anti-Scottish satire in *Eastward Ho!* (1605), a comedy he wrote with George Chapman and John Marston, with whom he was now reconciled. This time Jonson's aristocratic friends secured his release.

Jonson now began to write a new style of comedy, beginning with *Volpone* (1605–6). The play was a great success not only in London, but also on tour at Oxford and Cambridge universities. This was the recognition Jonson wanted, and in 1607 he dedicated a printed version of the play to both universities.

In 1607 he had his own house in Blackfriars, perhaps with his family again. The great 'middle comedies' continued with *Epicoene* (1609), *The Alchemist* (1610) and *Bartholomew Fair* (1614). He also wrote the Roman tragedy *Catiline* (1611) and a series of masques for the court. There was a spell as tutor to the son of Sir Walter Raleigh in 1612–13, but Jonson seemed to lack the necessary sobriety and sense of responsibility for the job, and a visit to Paris ended disastrously (*Conv.*, 245–53).

After *The Devil is an Ass* (1616) Jonson did not write for the stage for another ten years. He focused instead on his masques and his poetry. The year 1616 was an important one for him. A royal pension made him effectively the first Poet Laureate, and he published his collected poetry and selected masques and plays as if they were the text of a classical author: a folio volume entitled *The Works of Benjamin Jonson*. He was mocked by some at the time for his presumption. To publish plays in particular in this way was a bold assertion of the literary status of an art form not hitherto accorded such importance. It was also a landmark declaration of Jonson's own authority as the individual source of these works. An honorary doctorate from Oxford followed in 1619. Jonson was now a public celebrity, and gathered around him a group of admiring younger writers with whom he caroused in the London taverns, 'the tribe of Ben'. Both his own natural sons were dead.

Jonson's library was destroyed by fire in 1623, a serious blow to him. King James's son Charles, who came to the throne in 1625, did not require Jonson's services as frequently as his father. After a stroke in 1628 Jonson was more or less confined to his room in Westminster. He returned to play-writing, but now met little acclaim or commercial success. His final comedies were *The Staple*

1.1 Ben Jonson, after Abraham van Blyenberch, c.1617.
National Portrait Gallery.

of News (1626), *The New Inn* (1629), *The Magnetic Lady* (1632) and *A Tale of a Tub* (1634). After some difficult years early in the new reign his pension was renewed and increased in 1630. When he died in August 1637 he was buried, upright, in Westminster Abbey. He was still held in high public regard. Jonson's funeral was well attended by those noblemen and gentry still in London during the summer.

THE ROOTS OF JONSONIAN THEATRE: CLASSICISM AND HUMANISM

Jonson's career as a writer for the public stage is usually divided into three stages. In the early 'comical satires' he began to develop a theatrically complex, linguistically rich and morally prescriptive mode of writing with mixed results. In the middle period, from *Sejanus* (1603) to *The Devil is an Ass* (1616), the mature Jonson produced a series of remarkable plays, mostly comedies, which are the principal focus of this book. Their distinguishing features can be crudely listed as follows:

1. the precise and self-conscious use of a wide range of literary materials, drawn most often from Greek and Roman sources
2. an overt project to produce moral reflection through challenging the audience's beliefs and attitudes about both theatre and their own lives
3. an 'open' mode of representation where there is no clear boundary between the onstage world of the play and its characters, and the 'real' world of actors and audience
4. a sense of playfulness and delight about the whole project: a sense that actors and audience are engaged in a form of game, often a kind of practical joke at the expense of either certain characters or of the audience, or of both
5. topicality. The plays are firmly located in the moment of their production, especially in terms of contemporary politics and current events.

These five features are far less evident in the late plays (1626–37), which are much more conventional romantic comedies in many respects.

The roots of Jonson's theatre are to be found in the intellectual traditions to which he firmly adhered, and in his own varied and complex life in the society of early modern London.

These intellectual traditions are principally classicism and humanism. Jonson's immersion in Greek and Latin authors is obvious everywhere in his work. It would be wrong, however, to think that the classical writers were merely 'sources' upon which he drew. Jonson saw himself as part of the same unbroken literary and cultural tradition as his ancient forebears. Classical literature was an inheritance which remained valid in its responses to the contemporary world. As John Mulryan writes, 'classicism' 'asserts and celebrates the existence of a series of timeless, unvarying principles of conduct and thought: attention to form, decorum, knowledge, the past, imitation, consistency, fidelity, personal worth' (Mulryan 2000: 163). Classicism was a way of making sense of the world and of providing clear principles of thought, but it should not be thought that those principles always led to the same conclusions. As Mulryan suggests, classicism may well carry 'the connotation of conservative' (Mulryan 2000: 164), but there are many different strands of political thought in classical writing, from the libertarian and republican to the authoritarian.

As far as writing was concerned, Jonson's classicism asserted the primary importance of elegant form in the artwork, a form which expressed a content which imitated the substance of the finest classical models. In his prologue to *Volpone* Jonson proclaimed that:

> The laws of time, place, persons he observeth,
> From no *needful* rule he swerveth.
> (ll. 31–2; my emphasis)

He recognised both the elegance and the authority of the so-called unities and often adhered to them. (The unities derive broadly from Aristotle's *Poetics*, as developed by continental Renaissance theorists, and require that the action of a play should be contained in a single day and a single place, and have only one main narrative.) However, as in the case of *Volpone*, a play with six overlapping plots, Jonson is all too ready to adapt himself to what will work on the early modern stage. His earliest extant play, *The Case is Altered*, is perhaps the most obviously derived from a classical form, the comedies *Aulularia* and *Captivi* of Plautus. But even here, Jonson combined the plots of the two plays to produce 'intrigue and romance in such abundance that the utter improbability of it all would be obvious' (Cave 1991: 10). In doing so, suggests Richard Cave, he set out to make the audience laugh at their own desire for the superficial emotional consolations of Elizabethan comedy (Cave 1991: 10–11). In his tragedy *Sejanus*, Jonson's adaptation of the form to his own theatrical and didactic purposes is subtle but highly effective (see below, pp. 34–6; 41–5).

The formal elegance of the dramatic work always mattered more than adherence to the unities. The romantic critic S. T. Coleridge rated the plot of *The Alchemist* among 'the three best plots ever planned' (Holdsworth 1978: 149). Not only the ingenious perfection of the plotting, but the balance and distribution of action, and the requirement for different levels of pace and energy within the whole play and within individual scenes, are elements to which Jonson devotes great care. Even if onstage we watch what appears to be merely 'a series of colourful monstrous characters rushing on, with an underlying seriousness and drive', said the playwright Peter Barnes, 'if you go back to the text you can see how it's all be[en] slotted together' (Barnes et al. 1972: 25).

Drummond tells how Jonson thought that three books of the Roman rhetorician Quintilian were 'not only to be read, but altogether digested' (*Conv.*, ll. 105–6).[2] Jonson's commitment to the importance of classical rhetorical practice entailed paying even more attention to the patterns of sound and action in his work than was usual even in early modern drama. The physicality of the text transmits itself powerfully into performance (see below, p. 69).

The content of Jonson's plays draws on a huge range of classical and later authors, according to the play concerned. What may seem a little like plagiarism in the post-Romantic era was, in the Renaissance, adherence to the classical doctrine of *imitatio*. In his commonplace book Jonson used the analogy of eating. The classical writer imitates great writers 'not as a creature that swallows what it takes in crude, raw, or indigested, but that feeds with an appetite, and hath a stomach to concoct, divide and turn all into nourishment' (*Disc.*, ll. 2495–9).

Not only the words, but also the tone and approach of certain writers are subject to Jonson's transformative imitation. In the middle comedies the influence of the Greek writers Aristophanes and Lucian on Jonson's method is particularly evident. The comedies of the Athenian dramatist Aristophanes (c. 448–c. 380 BC) engage specifically with contemporary personalities and politics of the city. They are rumbustiously satirical, bawdy, energetic and linguistically flamboyant; above all there is a serious moral sensibility and a commitment to theatre as moral education. As a study of the Aristophanic influence on Jonson asserts, 'Jonson is Aristophanic in his effort to make men conscious of themselves, of others, and of the human values which preserve humanity' (Lafkidou Dick 1974: 10).[3] Lucian was a prose satirist who lived in Syria in the second century AD. His stories are playful farces, teasing the reader by making them laugh with delight at situations which undermine or confuse conventionally held moral views. The under-lying purpose was to encourage readers, through laughter, to examine their own ideas and preconceptions; Lucian saw himself as a kind of cross between Aristophanes and the provocative philoso-pher Socrates.

Indeed, as both a classicist and a humanist, Jonson often stated the moral purpose of theatre. The words of Jonson's favourite Latin poet, Horace, are often repeated in Jonson's prologues: 'to mix profit with your pleasure' (*Volp.*, Prol., l. 8). In the 'Epistle Dedicatory' which he addressed to the universities of Oxford and Cambridge as a preface to *Volpone* in 1607, he declared that it was 'the office of a comic poet [playwright] to imitate justice, and instruct to life, as well as purity of language and stir up gentle affections' (ll. 112–14). 'Imitate' here seems to mean 'representing' justice both in the sense of seeing justice done on stage and stand-ing up for what is right. But it can also mean to show justice as it imperfectly exists in the world now, so that we can strive to become more virtuous and to live in a more just world. In the prologue to *The Alchemist* Jonson declares that 'this pen/ Did never aim to grieve, but better men' (ll. 11–12). This does not mean, I think, that Jonson brought to his mature plays any rigid moral ideals against which the world was to be measured, as some have considered (Maus 1984: 5–6). The prologue goes on to suggest that his play is not a perfect, unchanging reflecting surface in what the Elizabethan poet Sir Philip Sidney called the 'golden world' of art (Sidney 1966: 24); nor Hamlet's mirror held up to the world 'to show virtue her feature, scorn her own image' (III, ii, 22–3). Jonson writes that:

> If there be any that will stir so nigh
> Unto the stream to look what it doth run,
> They shall find things they'd think, or wish were done.
>
> (ll. 20–2)

Jonson's theatre is a moving stream which reflects the world back to itself, a dynamic and constantly moving, fluctuating surface. Art is part of human experience and does not stand still outside time, but is part of historical change itself. The world in which Jonson lived was too complex and dynamic to assume that a simple basis for moral judgements is possible, a problem which his best plays both present and explore. But there is nevertheless such a thing as justice and a 'best reason of living' (*Volp.*, Ded., l. 101). Another significant classical influence was the writings of the Stoic philosophers, and of Seneca in particular. The Stoics believed virtue was possible but very hard to achieve indeed.

The morally efficacious purpose of art was an aspect of Greek and Roman thought also important in humanism. It is true that the impact of developing capitalism in Jacobean London can at times put 'Jonson's humanist vocabulary . . . under strain, fighting a rearguard action in the world' (Dutton 1996: 20), but it was an action that Jonson relished.

Humanism was an important intellectual movement in western Europe in the late fifteenth to the early seventeenth century. At its heart was a belief in the power of education to enable the naturally undetermined individual to fulfil the potential which God had made possible. Classical learning and the application of reason were the foundations of education, rather than mere authority or tradition. Yet humanism also stressed the dialectical conflict between precept and experience, and it is not surprising that drama was an important element in the humanist movement. Not only were the performance and writing of plays in schools and colleges, in both Latin and English, part of its educational project, but the playful, dialectical interaction which is at the heart of performance was consonant with their pluralistic manner of thought. There may well be a universal oneness in the mind of God, but the humanists' struggles with the intractable contradictions of human experience were informed by an awareness that experience, with all its contradictions, is all we have to go on. Kent Cartwright describes humanist drama of the sixteenth century in terms which sound more than a little like Jonsonian comedy. He notes 'its sense of lively play and unpredictability, manifested in linguistic exuberance, parody, physicality, virtuosic acting and teasing enigma' (Cartwright 1999: 2)

We know that Jonson was reading the central figure in English humanism, Desiderius Erasmus (c. 1467–1536), and in particular his *Praise of Folly* immediately before he wrote *Volpone*, when, according to David Riggs, he 'was rethinking his entire approach to comedy'. Riggs also finds plenty of evidence of the influence of Lucian's *Dialogues* in the middle comedies, and remarks that Erasmus praised Lucian 'for "reviving the sharpness of old comedy while stopping short of its abusiveness", and concluded that he knew of "no stage comedy or satire which can be compared with this man's dialogues"' (Riggs 1989: 135). Douglas Duncan concludes his study of the influence of Lucian and Erasmus on Jonson's dramatic writing as follows:

> Jonson sought to validate the theatre by making it a proving ground of virtue, a testing-place of judgement, worthy of the belief in the function of literature which he shared with the other humanists, after him as well as before.
>
> (Duncan 1979: 235)

In defending his *Colloquies* against the objections of the ecclesiastical authorities, Erasmus argued than 'nothing is better learned than what is learned as a game' [*quam quod ludendo discitur*].[4] And as a game, representation of a fictional world is not the prime concern. What marks out this particular mode of Erasmus's work, writes Duncan,

> is a basic distrust of fiction *per se*. For him, the imitation of life was still less an end in itself than the play of the mind. His characters and their actions are never essentially more than counters in the intellectual game he plays with his readers.
>
> (Duncan 1979: 50)

This game – *lusus* – for Erasmus had 'three closely related aspects':

The first of these is the surface quality of the game, the display of wit, which he regards as mainly responsible for producing *voluptas*, or pleasure. The second is the serious content or implication of the game, embodying *utilitas* or profit. The third aspect . . . is the rhetorical method involved, the intended impact on the reader as participant.

(Duncan 1979: 31)

Erasmus was writing prose fiction, but the primarily non-representational virtuosic display of wit and the careful impact on an audience who are participators are both typical characteristics of Jonson's middle comedies. The 'serious content or implication of the game' in these plays, however, develops the moral disorientation of Erasmus's most playful writing in a remarkably challenging way. Erasmus's *Praise of Folly* (1511) notoriously disorientates the reader as it moves between different voices and tones, at one time self-mocking, at another sharply and seriously satirical; serious in praising madness and lunacy at one moment, and then in indicting the follies of human life at another. There is no conclusion which enables readers to align themselves with the work's intended direction, but instead a dazzling display of wit and paradox.

Whatever Erasmus's religious purpose may have been, Jonson's intention is avowedly moral. The moral paradoxes of the middle comedies clearly do spring from the humanist idea of *serio ludere*, of a game where there is a serious moral point which is to be discerned with difficulty through the fallacies and twists and turns of the argument or narrative. But, if this is the case, then the traditional idea that Jonson is a simple and traditional conservative moralist is hardly in line with this tradition. Richard Cave makes a telling point that 'values in Jonson's mature comedies are usually conspicuous by their absence.' He goes on to suggest that *Epicoene*'s 'climactic act' is 'shocking the better to liberate' (Cave 1991: 71, 72; see below, p. 83).

Jonson's characteristic mode of theatrical representation also finds its roots in the humanist and popular drama of the sixteenth century. Some critics have identified Jonson with an interpretation of humanism which sees human nature and the categories of human conduct as fixed, standing outside the historical process. Robert Weimann argues that the humanist notion of dramatic representation sees the performance text as a smooth, perfect mirror which will reflect back to the real world its own deficiencies and endorse ruling-class values under the guise of 'universal' standards contained in the artistic form. The critics Pauline Kiernan (1996: 18–19), Achsah Guibbory (1986: 110–11) and Alexander Leggatt (1981: 44) accuse Jonson of just such neo-classicism. In such a mode of performance, the actor would be totally absorbed in the role, dwelling entirely in the formally self-contained world-of-the-play. But the actual practice of Jonson's best plays does not endorse this view at all, as the succeeding chapters will demonstrate.

As in Aristophanes' plays (see above, p. 10), the audience are participants in an event which explicitly acknowledges their presence and refers to events and personalities in contemporary London, even sometimes to the names of the actors on stage. The notion of play, of adopting a set of formal ground rules which are understood by everyone and which establish clearly that what is happening inside them is not to be taken in the same way as what happens outside them, may be useful here. In late medieval and Tudor drama 'play' or 'game' was the carefully crafted 'make-believe action presented by actors on a stage', as distinct from the 'earnest' of the 'spiritual or physical actuality' of the world (Wickham 1981: 67). Representation was emblematic, not mimetic, so that it was 'not properly speaking a representation at all. It's a game, something like a festival observance' (Womack 1986: 42).[5] Something of this pre-Reformation mode of representation lives on in Jonson. In English Catholic humanism there was a dialectic between 'sacramental/analogical thinking' which 'tend[ed] to deny rigid boundaries; nothing is simply itself, but things are signs of other things and one thing may be inside another', and a more rationalistic mode of thought which aimed to demarcate fixed categories in the world (Kuller Shuger 1990: 11). The Eucharist, which Catholics believe is Christ's flesh and blood whilst appearing to be bread and wine, was the most obvious and controversial example of the former; a Jonsonian actor is a further example.

Even though the characters in Jonson's great plays are usually behaving as if they were in a different reality, there is no doubt in the audience's minds or the actors' behaviour that they are all in the same world all the time. Jonson is not trying to depict the truth about the world. Rather, in the words of 'Another Prologue' to *Epicoene*, 'poet never credit gained/ By writing truths, but things, (like truths) well feigned' (ll. 9–10). In its context these lines indicate that Jonson is disguising his moral project as drama to make it palatable to his audience. But it also suggests that the mimetic project is sterile and unappealing, since drama cannot depict 'truth'. It cannot put 'real' people on stage; it would not be believable, be worthy of 'credit'. The moral challenge of the 'well-feigned' plays occurs in the same 'world' as the audience, not in a represented one which they observe at a distance.

There is also a presence of 'popular' theatre and its traditions in Jonson's comedies. This was evident to the critic William Archer who, in the 1920s, condemned the implausibility of *Volpone*, writing with an air of elitist *hauteur* that Jonsonian comedy came from a more primitive stage of cultural development, the stage of 'music halls and picture palaces', where the audience was active, not passive (Woolland 2002: 4). Brian Woolland points out how features common to Jonson's dramatic writing are still integral to popular entertainment today, and have passed into television comedy and drama. The multiple plots or series of rapid sketches, the grotesque characterisations, the contemporary references, an infectious delight in word-play, biting satire and a self-conscious mode of representation are as central to Jonson as they were to nineteenth-century music hall and twentieth-century revue, and are to twenty-first-century television comedy sketch shows.

Ben Jonson was taught at Westminster by one of the great humanist scholars. He went on to become, 'with the exception of John Milton', the most learned poet in the language, especially in the classics (Young 2000: 43). When he wrote *Sejanus* and the middle comedies he had been a bricklayer, a soldier and an actor, and was still a secret Catholic. All of these factors clearly had some role to play in the development of his distinctive theatrical style.

JONSON AND AUTHORITY

Jonson has some claim to be the first professional writer in English literature (Dutton 1996: 2). He wrote both for aristocratic patrons and for the commercial theatre. He also published his work, dedicated to the nobility, in order to make money. Sitting uneasily between these two camps, he nevertheless established himself as the individual originator of his writings, which was unusual enough. The title pages of printed Quartos distinguish between himself, the aristocratic patron (to whom the term 'author' had previously often applied) and the production which the actors had staged. *Every Man Out of His Humour* and *Sejanus* are examples (Dutton 1996: 25). At a time when commercial publication was not the act of a gentleman (Donne's *Songs and Sonnets*, for example, only ever circulated in manuscript in his lifetime), Jonson based his right to publish on his classical learning; his authority, in both senses of the word, was derived from these high-status ancients whose heir he proclaimed himself to be (Dutton 1996: 27). Jonson is often seen as the first bourgeois individualist author, asserting his identity as a competitive producer of a brand of writing that bears his name. Yet, given Jonson's critique of nascent capitalist consumerism, the 1616 Folio should perhaps rather be seen as an attempt to add to the classical canon: to be the last Horace, not the first Dickens.

There is also a critical opinion, particularly evident in twentieth-century American criticism, which sees Jonson as disdainful of the theatre (see, for example, Barish 1973b). Richard Dutton argues convincingly that this was not a snobbish condescension for a popular art form (Dutton 1996: 47–9), but rather a general unease about the fluid and unpredictable response of the crowd in a communal experience. In all of Jonson's dramatic writing he strives to guide the serious response of individuals in the audience to key issues of judgement, both moral and aesthetic. The process can be rather crude in the early and late plays, but in the middle period he shows enormous bravery and sophistication in his implication of the audience in the game of the play, not as festive participants, but compromised critics.

NOTES

1. Collinson (1995: 160) suggests that Jonson was in fact born in 1574, and that his father was the pugnacious Puritan

minister Robert Johnson, who died in the prison of Westminster Gatehouse that same year.
2. In 1618 the Scottish nobleman Drummond of Hawthornden made notes on Jonson's conversation during his stay with him. These 'Conversations' are a prime source for Jonson's life and opinions.
3. For an argument, based on Jonson's non-dramatic writings, that in his middle comedies Jonson abandoned the Aristophanic mode for that of classical 'New Comedy' see Dutton 1996: 109–12.
4. Quoted in Duncan 1979: 46. The idea is also Horatian: 'quamquam ridentem dicere verum/quid vetat' ['what can forbid speaking a truth with a laugh?'] (Satires, I, i, 24–5).
5. Womack in fact regards Jonsonian representation mostly as standing in contrast to such a mode of drama.

CHAPTER 2

The Early Comedies
(1597–1601)

Jonson told Drummond in 1618 that 'half of his comedies were not in print' (*Conv.*, l. 336). What survives of the work he wrote in the final years of Queen Elizabeth's reign is clearly different in quality from his great plays of the Jacobean era, but perhaps more interesting than the romances which he wrote under Charles I.

CONTEXTS

In these years Jonson strove to establish himself on the London literary scene, but not on any terms. The fruits of his friendship with the wits of the Inns of Court, including John Donne, can be seen in his popular exercise in the fashionable genre of satire, *Every Man Out of His Humour*, which seems to have been reprinted three times in 1600 (Kay 1995: 50). But Jonson's situation in such company was uneasy. He clearly felt uncomfortable with his own lack of 'gentility', and sought to elevate the role of honest scholar-poet in the comedies of 1598–1601; Jonson's right to criticise the manners of his social superiors was established by his learning and virtue.

This right was not recognised by all. The commercial publication of a playscript as serious literature was not the style of the gentleman amateur of the Inns of Court. There was a falling-out first of all with John Marston, an erstwhile friend and fellow playwright, himself the offspring of landed gentry. At some point, according to

Drummond, Jonson beat Marston 'and took his pistol' (*Conv.*, l. 235). Marston put a savage satire of Jonson on stage in his play *What You Will* (1601), in the character of 'Lampatho Doria', a self-regarding, book-obsessed idiot. Jonson discovered that another fellow-writer, Thomas Dekker, was working on a second attack and rapidly produced *Poetaster*, in which both Marston (Crispinus) and Dekker (Demetrius) are held up to ridicule before humiliation at the hands of Horace (Jonson). The Latin poet, himself of humble origins but a devotee of the plain style and high moral seriousness, was Jonson's model among the ancients. Dekker's *Satiromastix; or the Untrussing of the Humorous Poet* (1601) cruelly lampooned 'Horace' as a quarrelsome, ugly hack who is ultimately humiliated by being stripped of his satyr costume by the courtiers.[1] Jonson's response was an 'Apologetical Dialogue' as an accompaniment to *Poetaster*, which was only spoken once on stage before being banned by the authorities. This ended the so-called *Poetomachia* or 'War of the Theatres'.[2]

Jonson seems to have established himself on the public stages with the success of his two 'humour' comedies, *Every Man In His Humour* (1598) and, in particular, *Every Man Out of His Humour* (1599). When the vogue for published prose and verse satire seemed to the authorities to be getting out of hand it was banned by the Bishop of London and the Archbishop of Canterbury in June 1599. George Chapman's *An Humorous Day's Mirth* (1597) had already transferred the satirist's mockery of contemporary character types to the stage. Jonson then drew on this fashionable subject and produced innovative and distinctive drama in the only literary form in which satire was permitted.

The four 'humours' of ancient medicine were bodily fluids (blood, phlegm, choler and black bile). A preponderance of one would supposedly lead to a dominant character trait in an individual, who might be sanguine, phlegmatic, angry or melancholic. As Jonson's mouthpiece Asper expresses it in the prologue of *Every Man Out of His Humour*:

> When some peculiar quality
> Doth so possess a man that it doth draw
> All his affects, his spirits and his powers,

> In their confluctions all to run one way;
> This may be truly said to be a humour.
>
> (ll. 105–9)

In these two plays, it might seem, the dénouement serves to 'cure' many of the characters of their humour by exposing them to public ridicule. When it was the critical fashion to berate Jonson for his inability to produce 'convincing' psychological characterisation in the manner of Shakespeare, Jonson's supposed adherence to the crude and mechanistic view of the human mind represented by humours theory was often cited and applied to his plays in general.[3] Such anachronistic criticism, which would seek to praise drama in so far as it approaches the condition of a novel, was always misplaced. In these early plays, and later, Jonson does not seek to mirror the world but to make his audience actively reflect upon their own conduct and upon the conduct of those in positions of responsibility in society, not just those characters who appear on stage.

It is never wise, however, to take Jonson's own theoretical explanation of his practice at face value. Robert N. Watson points out that in *Every Man In His Humour* 'Jonson's characters are driven less by chemistry than by fantasy; they are less what they eat than what they read' (Jonson 1998b: xiii). The play's boastful soldier is only pretending to be brave, and the melancholic poetry-writing lover is a plagiarist affecting that role. Jonson is satirising, on stage, characters who construct their personalities from literary and theatrical models. Even in these early plays the interpenetration of the offstage and onstage worlds is a prime concern.

THE CASE IS ALTERED (1597)

Jonson's earliest surviving play was written for Lord Pembroke's men when the playwright was still an actor himself. *The Case is Altered* is in many respects a conventional Elizabethan comedy concerning the romantic and familial misunderstandings and misadventures of a group of Italian aristocrats, punctuated by comic scenes featuring their foolish servants. Jonson's sources were not to be found on the contemporary stage, however, but in the Roman 'New Comedy' from which Elizabethan comedy was itself derived. Jonson merged *Captivi* ('The Captives') and *Aulularia* ('The Pot of Gold') by the Roman comic playwright Plautus (c. 254-184 BC). Neither play had yet been translated into English.

Count Ferneze of Milan is very concerned for the safety of the son on whom he dotes, Paulo, who is off to fight the French. Ferneze had lost his infant son Camillo when the French captured Vicenza, years before. Paulo is taken prisoner, but a French lord, Chamont, and his commoner friend, Gasper, are brought back as captives to Milan. Ferneze sends 'Gasper' off to effect an exchange of Chamont for Paulo, only to discover that Gasper has been impersonating the Lord. The distraught Count sets an ultimatum for the return of his son and is on the point of killing Gasper himself in retribution when he is stayed by some kind of vision (V, ix, 22-8). Chamont suddenly returns with Paulo, and Ferneze's joy is complete when a chance remark leads to Chamont's realisation that Gasper is in fact Paulo's long-missing brother Camillo.

The romantic plot strand concerns the five different men who seek the hand of Rachel du Prie. They include Paolo, Ferneze himself and his servant Christophero. Rachel's father Jacques has kept her out of the way of suitors but believes that the men are after not his daughter but rather his hoard of gold, which he hides under a heap of manure for safety. He is lured away from his house by a trail of gold coins laid by one of Rachel's unscrupulous suitors, Angelo, who then attempts to rape Rachel before being prevented by Paulo's timely arrival. The gold is discovered and stolen by two servants, Onion and Juniper. Rachel turns out to be Chamont's lost sister.

Because of its dependence on Plautus the play is often compared to Shakespeare's own early play *The Comedy of Errors* (1592-4), but *The Case is Altered* offers no similar emotional satisfaction at its close. In the final scenes three lost children are recovered and a pauper girl is revealed as a noblewoman in a most perfunctory manner. Rachel says nothing in the final two scenes, and after so much passion Ferneze's response to the good news seems very lame (V, xi, 49-50). The effect of this is so startling after the success of the rest of the writing that critics feel that Jonson is deliberately sending up the conventional comic resolution. Richard Cave suggests that Jonson had hoped that the audience would laugh at the 'sheer artifice' of the conclusion, and in doing so 'would be laughing at their own susceptibilities and their desire for a theatre offering emotional consolations' (Cave 1991: 11). The fact that the material which Jonson inserted into the text before its Quarto publication in 1609 castigates the audiences for their unthinking philistinism (I, ii, II, vii, 26–82) would indicate that their hopes were unfounded. Cave finds in both Ferneze and Jacques a dangerous, deeply drawn obsession that comes close to tragedy, challenges the audience and makes them 'question the ground on which they have been laughing at these two characters' (Cave 1991: 14). In this the play looks forward to the achievement of the later plays.

Robert L. Mack finds another pointer to the future, in Ferneze's unsuitability as an authority figure in the play. This produces a 'realization that all authority is perhaps arbitrary – or at least a discomfort for those who stand in a judgemental position over others' (Mack 1997: 56), an insight which looks forward to the ideas of the middle comedies. The conflation of gold with ordure in the Jacques plot may or may not be an ill-disguised attack on Robert Brett, Jonson's bricklayer stepfather who built a garden over a sewer (Riggs 1989: 30–1). But it does anticipate Jonson's attitude to gold in *Volpone* and *The Alchemist*.

I am not aware that *The Case is Altered* has been performed professionally since the Jacobean period.

EVERY MAN IN HIS HUMOUR (1598)

Two different texts exist for this comedy. The earliest version, published as a Quarto in 1601, is set in Florence, but a Florence that seems much more like London. Jonson revised the play, probably in 1612, but perhaps earlier (Barton 1984: 45; Haynes 1992: 34). The version which is published in the 1616 Folio (see above, p. 5) is dense with references to the capital city where it now takes place. English names which indicate the personalities of many characters have replaced the Italian ones. The following brief discussion will be of the Folio text, except where useful comparisons can be drawn.

The plot of *Every Man In His Humour*, such as it is, very loosely draws on the conventions of Roman New Comedy. For some reason old Edward Knowell wants to make sure that his son young Edward is not led astray by the gallant wastrel Wellbred and sets off into the city to follow him to Wellbred's lodgings. Wellbred lives with the merchant Kitely, a man manically jealous about his wife, Wellbred's sister. Old Edward's cunning servant Brainworm adopts various disguises to ensure that young Edward's path is clear to marry Kitely's sister by the end of the play. Different strands of the plot come together in Act IV scene x where Kitely, his wife and Old Edward arrive at the house of Cob the water-bearer. Inside is Cob's wife Tib, who becomes the centre of multiple mistaken accusations of infidelity. After confused recriminations they all set off to seek Justice Clement. Also seeking justice from the jovial magistrate are a group of characters whose general stupidity has been the main focus of the audience's attention and amusement: Stephen the fool from the country and Matthew the fool from the town, who thinks 'his' poetry can win Bridget's hand; Downright the 'plain squire'; and Captain Bobadill, the braggart soldier and fencing master whose character comprises one of the play's principal delights.

Social and moral commentary drives the play, not narrative. What gives unity to the play, and most explicitly to the Folio text, is not the plot but the unity of time itself in its depiction of a day in a great city (Barton 1984: 46). Jonathan Haynes has compared Jonson's anchoring of his play in London to Joyce's use of Dublin in *Ulysses* (Haynes 1992: 35). The play follows the routines of the day, 'from the early morning distribution of fresh water from the conduits [I, iv], sordid awakenings in small lodging houses [I, v]', through the day to 'desultory talk in taverns and ordinaries, to supper and bed. The city is the true centre of the comedy and, to a large extent, its main character' (Barton 1984: 46).

The focus of the satire is on those who would aspire to the condition of gentleman but who prove inadequate; this is the major status division in the text and it is a 'tense and conflicted one' (Haynes 1992: 35). The play features the word 'gentleman' over a hundred times in both versions (Cave 1991: 20). The marriage plot is a mere framework on which hangs this examination of gentlemanly status in a dissolute and pretentious urban world. The older generation of Knowell and Kitely do not function in the comedy as conventional blocks to young romance, but rather as barriers to young Knowell and Wellbred's 'immersion in the milieu of social climbers' (Haynes 1992: 38). Status in this milieu is established not by birth, but by affectation in fashion (e.g. I, v, 70–7), by manner of speaking (I, iv, 69–73) or by smoking (I, iv, 73–7) – a 'humour'. But the true gentleman in this play, young Knowell, has acquired a 'connoisseur's sense for the new varieties of urban style' and knows well how to 'play with them, which often means playing *on* them sadistically' (Haynes 1992: 42). Such a man, relatively new in the theatre, can stand above the troubled emotions of the city where ubiquitous market exchange has rendered everything fluid; 'the productive value of his wit comes into its own as the dramatic mastery of a particular, unpredictable set of circumstances' (Hutson 1989: 12). Such a dramatic protagonist not only validated the new delight in the consumerist economy of London's wealthy elite, but stood for the theatre itself, an *arriviste* institution whose essential fluidity and witty social commentary from an elevated position echoed the embrace by the contemporary aristocracy of capitalist London. Satirical wit is itself the commodity on which the theatre trades. The urban gallant in the later plays will mutate from this young man of wit and judgement into a crueller and darker figure, as the romance of the market fades: Dauphine in *Epicoene* and Quarlous in *Bartholomew Fair*.

There is also a traditional virtue which the play proposes: the value of real poetry. In the final scene Justice Clement orders Matthew's 'works' to be burned. They had already been exposed by young Edward Knowell as plagiarised from Marlowe's 'Hero and Leander' (IV, ii, 39). When a crude version of one of Daniel's 'Delia' sonnets is read, the Justice concludes that 'here was enough to have infected the whole City' (V, v, 27–8), and goes on to stress the value of poets above magistrates (V, v, 33–8). In the Quarto version a speech in defence of poetry by young Edward goes further (a speech which was inserted into the 1986 Royal Shakespeare Company (RSC) performance of the Folio): 'nothing can more adorn humanity' than the 'reverend name' of 'true poet' (Jonson 1986: 74; HSS III: 286). Satire surprisingly gives way to a sincere, explicit and provocative assertion of the importance of poetry to the moral and political health of the city. It is a manifesto which this play will not put into convincing practice, but which serves as a marker for the future.

In production the intensity of Kitely's jealousy has impressed audiences and stood in contrast to the satirical mood and style of the rest of the play. *Every Man In His Humour* is the only one of Jonson's early plays to be revived professionally in the twentieth century (three times; see Jensen 1985: 36–40). Henry Goodman took the role for the RSC in 1986–7:

> [Goodman] addressed the many questions that make up Kitely's soliloquies and define his mental turmoil ... to specific members of the audience. We were being privileged with his most private confidences and yet we laughed. And with every guffaw his eyes grew wider with fright and desperation: we were insulting his dignity and not taking his anguish seriously; worse, he began to suspect that we were conniving at his wife's antics behind his back.
>
> (Cave 1991: 26)

Goodman was 'a delight', 'a master of paranoia'.[4] Goodman's insight again anticipates a feature of Jonson's mature comedies: the moral implication of the audience in cruelty. Even so, the production had mixed reviews. Its lack of narrative drive and cast of 'preposterous posers' meant that unsympathetic reviewers found it 'baffling and tedious', and requiring 'the audience's tolerance'.[5] The comedy has a precise focus on London morals in 1598 without the consistent brilliance of language and dramatic technique of the middle comedies.

EVERY MAN OUT OF HIS HUMOUR (1599) AND *CYNTHIA'S REVELS* (1600)

Never revived in modern times, Jonson's next play takes plotlessness and satirical fervour even further. In *Every Man Out of His Humour* cutting depictions of a range of the poseurs to be found in late Elizabethan London are put on display. In the words of Jonson's characterisation in the dramatis personae which prefaces the Folio version of the play, they include a 'vainglorious knight' (Puntarvolo, l. 12), a 'public, scurrilous and profane jester' (Carlo Buffone, l. 21), a 'neat, spruce affecting courtier' (Fastidius Brisk, l. 31), Deliro, who is 'a fellow sincerely besotted on his own wife' (l. 42), the 'proud mincing peat' Fallace (l. 51), and finally Shift, 'a threadbare shark', whose 'profession is skeldering and odling' [begging and cheating] (ll. 74–5). Once each character's humour has been clearly established and lampooned before the audience by some of the others, each is publicly exposed as a liar or hypocrite and thus put 'out of his humour'. That sums up the main action of the drama.

It is a brutal process, helped on its way by the embittered scholar Macilente, who cannot accept how fools can prosper in the world while the virtuous are scorned without an 'envious apoplexy' (l. 9). Macilente kills Puntarvolo's dog because ''twere the only true jest in the world' (V, i, 63). Buffone's mouth is sealed with hot wax (V, vi, 71). Brisk is left to languish in a debtor's prison to Macilente's delight (V, xi, 44–6), at the instigation of the heartbroken Deliro, who caught him embracing his chastened wife Fallace (V, x, 35). Shift, accused by Puntarvolo of stealing his dog, collapses to his knees in terror and admits his claim to be a highwayman to be lies (V, iii, 59–60).

Anne Barton has called the play 'conspicuously brilliant as well as . . . infuriating' (1984: 63). Jonson tore up all the conventions of Elizabethan comedy and produced something which was again closer to a revue sketch show. There were three Quarto texts published in 1600, which testifies to its popularity. Their title pages declare that they contain 'more than hath been publicly spoken or acted' (Barton 1984: 65). If the play possesses any brilliance, it may perhaps reside in the baroque excesses of its affected language, but more convincingly in its meta-theatrical boldness the play acknowledges and examines its own theatricality. There is a permanent onstage 'Grex' or chorus, consisting of Cordatus and Mitis. Mitis makes dim, conventional observations on the play and Cordatus, defending Jonson's artistic decisions, puts him in his place. In the play's Induction we meet Asper, the actor who plays Macilente, and the author of the play. He sets out his intentions to scourge the time's iniquities with characteristic fury: 'my strict hand/ Was made to seize on vice' (ll. 143–4). On the surface the audience seem to be being very firmly directed by both Induction and Grex how to interpret the play both morally and artistically, but Jonson's dramaturgy is more subtle than this. For the first time a Jonsonian examination of the nature of theatrical representation is taking place, hand in hand with an exploration of moral judgement in the theatre.

In putting on the stage an audience who explicitly interpret the play in the way in which the author intended Jonson is dramatising the conditions in which the play is judged and holding that act of judgement itself up to the scrutiny of the audience. This is 'a play which is about its own reception' (Loxley 2002: 51). The play's central scenes (III, i–vi) have been brilliantly analysed by Helen Ostovich as demonstrating Jonson's concern to foreground the theatre's own 'process of repression and selection' of 'reality' when it constructs a dramatically effective scene (Ostovich 1999: 77). Jonson's technique ensures that we see several conflicting perspectives at once in these scenes, in a very funny sequence which exposes the artifice of 'artistic unity of action and expression', and frees us from the 'subjective tunnel-vision, which Jonson satirizes as "humours"' (Ostovich 1999: 83, 81). The major section of Act III is set in Paul's Walk, the central aisle of the old St Paul's Cathedral, a space used as an informal market place, labour exchange and promenade for ostentatious display. In this familiar space Jonson offers a literal choreography of the vacuous gallants as they parade in groups which form and reform in a single dramatic sequence. They traduce each other out of earshot, as the Grex looks on. The precise dance-like movements required by the text operate 'in order to shift the audience out of social realism into an almost surreal vision of the new mercenary ethic' (Ostovich 1999: 78).

Two characters appear only in these scenes. Clove and Orange put on an act to try to impress the fashionable Paul's walkers, but soon realise that no one is listening to them and drop the act (III, iv, 34–5). It is a joke which encourages meta-theatrical reflection on the layers of performance and artifice which comprise the audience, the Grex, the gallants, Clove and Orange – but also the 'real' world of social display that is depicted. The explicit blurring of the boundaries between onstage and offstage is a feature of this play, for the first time in Jonson's work. An actor refuses to play the Prologue in the Induction (ll. 280–98); Macilente speaks in the final scene simultaneously as himself and Asper (V, xi, 68–71); and the presence of Puntarvolo's doomed dog onstage, resolutely itself and never in role but part of the action, has the same theatrical effect.

In the early Globe performances of the play Macilente's vitriolic humour was driven from him by the appearance of Queen Elizabeth before him. Jonson's next play, *Cynthia's Revels*, also relies on the Queen's appearance, this time as the allegorised Cynthia, to bring to an end the brazen parade of self-love of a group of idle courtiers and to sanction their subsequent penances in the fictional land of Gargaphie. *Cynthia's Revels* was written for a boy company at the private Blackfriars theatre. Its characters bear Greek names which identify their characters, and the gods Mercury and Cupid appear disguised. The play having even less plot than *Every Man Out of His Humour*, its characters spend their time playing various games. Its version of Macilente is the much-abused scholar Crites, who is eventually authorised by Cynthia to devise a masque which exposes the courtiers by making them impersonate virtues easily confused with their vices. But there is no general recognition on their part of their failings. *Cynthia's Revels* is not in any sense powerful dramatic writing; Tom Cain has called it 'shapeless and complacent' (Jonson 1995: 34). It does not seem to have been revived since its poorly received court performance, and has received little critical attention.

POETASTER (1601)

Jonson's final shot in the *Poetomachia* was written for the Children of the Chapel Royal, also at what was then the private Blackfriars playhouse. The play is set very precisely in the Rome of the Emperor Augustus, and is packed with long quotations from Latin literature which the students of the Inns of Court who frequented this playhouse would recognise. Much more carefully constructed than the other comical satires, *Poetaster* – the name means a 'petty or paltry poet' (Jonson 1995: 62) – puts on stage many of the leading poets of this 'golden age' of Latin literature and holds them up for judgement.

Ovid, whose father, like Old Knowell, hopes his son will abandon poetry for the law, organises a fancy-dress party where citizens and poets imitate the banquet of the gods in Book I of Homer's *Iliad*, but which turns into a prelude to adultery (IV, v, 22–36). The informer and tribune Lupus leads the Emperor to break up the revelry. Augustus furiously threatens his daughter Julia, and then exiles her admirer Ovid for his part in the romp. The poet Horace advises clemency but is disregarded. Elsewhere Horace is portrayed as a man of tact, wisdom and excellent judgement, even when provoked by the self-regarding and envious Crispinus, a comic representation of Jonson's rival John Marston. Horace is, of course, to be taken as Jonson himself.

At a reading of Virgil's masterpiece the *Aeneid* Augustus invites this most valued poet of all to take the emperor's chair, since

> Virtue without presumption place may take
> Above best kings, whom only she should make.
>
> (V, ii, 26–7)

This contrasting entertainment is interrupted by Lupus, who accuses Horace of seditious libel. Horace refutes him and Caesar orders the tribune to be gagged. Crispinus and Demetrius (Dekker) are then arraigned for plagiarism and calumny against Horace. The work of both is parodied and ridiculed, and Horace makes Crispinus swallow a pill which causes him to vomit up the absurd Latinate vocabulary in which Marston delighted ('O – glibbery – lubrical – defunct – O – ') (V, iii, 426).

Poetaster displays a concern for the conditions of its own reception and representational strategies (Cave 2003: 13) which will come to be hallmarks of the later plays. Lupus' accusations against Horace hinge on the interpretation of an emblem – an allegorical picture with a motto – which the poet was designing. Peter Womack argues that it is the authority of the Emperor which is the final arbiter of meaning in the drama. It is Caesar's arrival at the banquet that ends the ambiguity of the partygoers' identities; 'the repressive presence of the monarch re-fixes the identities briefly loosened by play' (Womack 1986: 110). At a time when informers could reinterpret a speaker's words to a government paranoid about Catholic subversion, and when strict slander laws could entail prison, and worse, for a writer of a play which could be 'applied' to powerful living men, Jonson may be seen to be living out a fantasy of univocal representation guaranteed by royal authority.

Womack comments on how the destruction of the fancy-dress party constitutes an attack on the idea of theatre, for the actor scandalously possesses two identities, neither fixed in performance. Tom Cain and Katharine Maus (1984: 90) suggest that 'Jonson consistently equates Ovidian metamorphosis with vice . . . a highly problematic attitude for a dramatist, dependent on the metamorphoses of actors' (Jonson 1995: 21). But Womack's argument depends on an account of Jonson as a proto-Enlightenment figure, rather than a classical humanist with a belief in the mysterious doubleness of existence (see above, pp. 11, 13–14). A fancy-dress party is not, in any case, theatre. Caesar's action is not presented as worthy of unambiguous approval. He behaves with unwarranted savagery when he breaks up the revels and tries to kill his own daughter (IV, vi, 11–16). Horace and Maecenas, poet and patron of poets, prevent him. Jonson, unlike his critics, does not conflate theatrical and verbal representation. The conscious ambiguity of the former renders it an inapt analogue for precise linguistic communication. If Jonson were the anti-theatricalist he is claimed to be, why did he expend so much energy writing such exciting theatre?

Jonson's commitment to a verbal language which communicates clearly goes with a commitment to a responsible civic discourse (Loxley 2002: 56), where individuals could put their trust in each other and the commonwealth, in the model of the idealised Roman polity. Ovid is to be condemned for misusing a powerful political discourse for erotic pleasure. His last, misguided couplet is:

> The truest wisdom silly [happy, innocent] men can have
> Is dotage on the follies of their flesh.
>
> (IV, x, 108–9)

The play's classicism asks its audience to take seriously the values which were the basis of the Elizabethan educational system and hold them up in comparison with their own society. *Poetaster* has a clear and demanding political vision. Furthermore, as Richard Cave also argues:

To appreciate its subtlest effects, the play invites spectators who are *in the know*; but, typical of Jonson, the result both flatters and challenges their specialist knowledge. His audience cannot sit back, confident in their superior insight: they are required to observe and judge.

(Cave 2003: 20)

Poetaster lacks dramatic intensity because it is so straightforward, if not ascetic, in its moral positions; it 'lacks the element of danger which characterises Jonson's comedy at its finest' (Cave 1991: 18); 'instinct and appetite are not seen as vital and positive . . . but as limiting' (Jonson 1995: 13). Yet it also possesses a superb comic creation in the form of the slippery, baroque-tongued and irresistibly larger than life skelderer, Pantilius Tucca, who anticipates future comic creations.

NOTES

1. Presumably an insulting allusion to the half-man half-goat Marsyas, who was flayed by Apollo for supposing himself the god's superior as a musician.
2. For the idea that Shakespeare in fact had the last word with Malvolio in *Twelfth Night* see Riggs 1989: 84–5.
3. See, for example, the introduction to David Cook's 1962 edition of *Volpone* (Jonson 1962: 21–4).
4. Charles Osborne in the *Daily Telegraph*, 13 April 1987; Nicholas de Jongh in *The Guardian*, 15 April 1987.
5. David Shannon in *Sunday Today*, 19 April 1987; Steve Grant in *Time Out*, 22 April 1987; Milton Shulman in the *Evening Standard*, 14 April 1987.

CHAPTER 3

The Roman Tragedies – *Sejanus* (1603) and *Catiline* (1611)

*S*ejanus was not Jonson's first attempt at tragedy. *Richard Crookback* (1602) is lost, together with his contribution to a collaboration with Chettle, Dekker and Marston, *Robert II*. Jonson's 1602 'additions' to Kyd's *The Spanish Tragedy* (1592) survive in the only version of that play to have come down to us. The two tragedies set in ancient Rome which he chose to include in the 1616 Folio enjoyed high repute among seventeenth-century intellectuals (Jonson 1990: 22–3; Riggs 1989: 178–9), it seems, but after disastrous opening public performances have rarely been performed since.

CONTEXTS

Sejanus caused Jonson to be summoned to appear before the royal Privy Council accused of 'popery and treason' (*Conv.*, l. 273). The content of the play could easily be construed as alluding to the falls of two recent royal favourites (Essex in 1601 and Raleigh in 1602–3) (Jonson 1990: 16–22; Riggs 1989: 105–6; Kay 1995: 72–3). We cannot, however, be sure of the exact grounds of the charge. The first text we possess of the play is the 1605 Quarto. This edition is all Jonson's work, unlike the original version which was a collaboration, probably with George Chapman. All the offending material seems to have been excised.

The 1605 Quarto goes to great lengths to indicate all of the classical texts upon which Jonson drew for each section of the play. His principal source for the story of the rise and fall of the over-reaching favourite of the Emperor Tiberius, Aelius Sejanus, was the *Annals* of the Roman historian Tacitus (AD 56–117). The *Annals*, notes W. David Kay, 'was read in the early seventeenth century either as a manual of state intrigue or as a warning against tyranni-cal rule' (Kay 1995: 71).[1] Tacitus looked back with world-weary pessimism at the dynasty which had snuffed out the last vestiges of republican freedom. He wished to record the political double-dealing, ruthless hypocrisy and cruelty of the Julio-Claudian emperors. A historian's duty, he wrote, was 'to ensure that merit be recorded, and to confront evil deeds and words with the fear of pos-terity's denunciation' (Tacitus 1989: 150).[2] Tacitus' *Annals* and the writing of those contemporary historians who emulated his manner came to be associated with discontented factions in the courts of both Elizabeth and James in the opening years of the seventeenth century. Jonson's source was therefore associated with a contempo-rary critique of tyrannical rule and Machiavellian politics.[3]

It might then be thought that Jonson supplied such a wealth of footnotes to his classical sources in the 1605 Quarto to demonstrate that *Sejanus* is principally a drama of precise historical reconstruc-tion in order that its author might escape further dangerous 'appli-cations' being made by agents of the government. In fact Jonson deviates significantly from his sources in the narrative to tell his own story (Jonson 1990: 28–37; Dutton 1978). In his own address to his readers in the Quarto Jonson promises that he has 'discharged the . . . office of a tragic writer' (l. 18), not that of a chronicler. Sejanus is far better understood not as a 'history play', but as the classical tragedy which Jonson says he set out to write.

Anne Barton has identified the crucial influence of the Greek comic dramatist Aristophanes in the development of Jonson's comic writing at this point in his career (Barton 1984: 113–14). In Aristophanes' *Frogs* Jonson would have read that the function of the tragic poet is 'to save the city' (Aristophanes 1964: 208).[4] Jonson's reading of the tragedies of Euripides in particular would also have suggested that the tragic poet acts as a particular kind of moral edu-cator to his society.[5] Athenian tragedy was not narrowly didactic in inculcating a single moral, political or religious doctrine, but encouraged its audience to reflect upon their own moral and political preconceptions and fundamentally re-examine them. It was, Paul Cartledge writes, 'genuinely a theatre of ideas, within a culture not the least remarkable attribute of which was a capacity to encompass the most radical critiques of social mores and cultural norms within a stable institutional framework' (Cartledge 1997: 21). Moreover, it was an art form which constantly examined its own means of communication to its audience.[6] Jonson's preface to *Sejanus* may boast of its facility in tragic style and decorum ('To the Readers', ll. 16–18), but the play may be usefully understood as an authentic classical tragedy in its didactic and meta-theatrical modes, which might still appeal to a contemporary audience (ibid., ll. 9–13).

Jonson was even closer to his classical sources in the later tragedy *Catiline*, principally Sallust's *On the Conspiracy of Catiline* and the speeches which the consul Cicero made to attack the Roman nobleman Lucius Sergius Catilina who attempted to seize power in a bloody coup in 63 BC. *Catiline* is a much more conventional classical tragedy than *Sejanus*, featuring as it does a chorus of sorts and a prologue by a ghost in the manner of Seneca. Why Jonson returned to classical tragedy at the height of his powers as a comic dramatist is unclear. There are clear allusions in the text to the Gunpowder Plot of 1605, connecting Catiline and his confederates to the Catholic extremists who tried to assassinate the King and parliament (see Kay 1995: 121–4). Since it seems likely that Jonson was forced by a new law to become once more a practising Anglican at this time (Riggs 1989: 176) and abandon his Catholicism, it may be that the Ciceronian, not Tacitean tragedy was intended to demonstrate his ultimate loyalty to the King and his ministers.

THE PLAYS

Jonson admitted that *Sejanus* lacked that essential feature of classical tragedy, 'a proper chorus'. The problem is that their 'habit and moods are such, and so difficult, as not any [playwright] since the Ancients' had succeeded in putting one on stage effectively ('To the

Readers', ll. 6–8). The function of the Greek chorus, a modern critic has observed, was not mere narrative, nor even to speak with a single voice, but 'to help the audience *become involved in the process of responding*, which may be a matter of dealing with profoundly contradictory impulses' (Easterling 1997: 164; author's emphasis). The choruses of Seneca's Roman tragedies, dramas which many lines of *Sejanus* consciously echo, fulfilled the same dramatic purpose. This is also the function as played by Mitis and Cordatus in *Every Man Out of His Humour*.

In *Sejanus*, the de facto chorus is a group of characters who form the ineffective opposition to the Emperor Tiberius, his favourites and cronies. This group is sometimes known as the 'Germanicans', as they are political associates of Agrippina, the widow of the murdered Germanicus, a nobleman of the imperial family whose virtue made him the hope of virtuous Romans dreaming of the 'freedom' of the long-gone republic.

Sejanus opens with two of this faction, Sabinus and Silius, lamenting a state where spies and informers work for the destruction of honest men, and where servile flattery brings political advancement. They are joined by others during the first act as they watch the henchmen of the Emperor's corrupt favourite Sejanus at work. They give their opinions of the Emperor's dissolute son Drusus, an enemy of Sejanus, and then watch Sejanus arrange to see and then meet Eudemus, the Greek physician who serves Drusus' wife Livia. Sejanus employs the Greek to 'affect' Livia with his love (I, 350), and then confides in the audience that this will be his means of destroying his rival for power, Drusus himself. Immediately after this the Emperor and his son enter. Tiberius inveighs against flatterers and refuses the Senate's offer for temples to be built for him. But he approves the erection of a statue of Sejanus, offering the Germanicans ample opportunity to comment on the disingenuous cunning of the Emperor. They then witness an enraged Drusus strike Sejanus – but not the favourite's final soliloquy in which he promises vengeance.

Thus the first act sets up the performance dynamic which will constitute Jonson's assimilation of classical tragedy into his own representational practice. Like the classical chorus, the Germanicans are onstage observers of the main action, offering commentary to the audience, albeit exclusively of a morally conventional nature. But unlike the classical chorus, they do not intervene with advice for the protagonist, nor address the audience directly in extended odes. Not only is it Sejanus himself who has the theatrical advantage of engaging directly with the audience; in this play the protagonists set out to destroy the chorus and deny its members a position from which moral responses can be made. When Drusus strikes Sejanus he is attempting to join the play's main action. Sejanus' only speech to him asks him simply to get out of his way (I, 563). Sejanus disregards the subsequent blow altogether.

The critic Katherine Eisaman Maus has suggested that Jonson's admiration for Stoic morality at this time creates a problem for the play's dramatic structure. The 'good and wise men' in the play (the Germanicans Arruntius, Silius, Cordus and Sabinus) have no 'control over their environment; they are every one of them politically impotent' (Maus 1984: 32). In fact Jonson has found a perfect theatrical realisation of Stoic political disengagement by making his Stoics a kind of classical chorus. But unlike a classical chorus, the main action of the play sets about silencing them, not least by the protagonists having more direct engagement with the audience than they can achieve.

Not that the audience are allowed to see much of the crucial action in this play. At the beginning of Act II, Livia is already won over by Sejanus, and in a scene remarkable for its subtle interplay between the language of a lady's cosmetics and the discourse of a murderous, megalomaniac politics, we discover that the adulterous lovers have suborned Eudemus to poison Drusus. In the following soliloquy Sejanus promises the audience that 'a race of wicked acts/ Shall flow out of my anger' (II, 151–2) and, in a rhetorical commonplace, suggests that the gods themselves are only the projection of men's fears (II, 161–2). Anne Barton writes of Sejanus in soliloquy that he talks 'only to himself' and 'never reveals an inner being with whom it is possible to sympathize, or even take seriously'; Brian Woolland says that he makes no attempt to get the audience ' "on side" ' since they are 'beneath Sejanus's contempt' (Barton 1984: 97; Woolland 2003: 32). Since Barton and Woolland wrote, the tragedy has been professionally staged for the first time since

1928 (see below, p. 50). One of the revelations of Gregory Doran's 2005–6 RSC production was the discovery of the ferocious sensual energy of Sejanus.[7] In the title role William Houston spoke his soliloquies directly to the audience, seeking not our approval indeed, but our admiration at his daring and at the depth of his appetites (see Fig. 3.1). In the RSC production this particular soliloquy was delivered to the audience as Sejanus buggered a male prostitute. He was always to be taken seriously and his sheer energy could not be ignored. As with Volpone or Mosca, to search for an inner being, such as one might find revealed in a Shakespearean soliloquy, is to miss the point. Sejanus is a pure theatrical phenomenon who sets out to challenge our conventional moral and political responses.

The Germanicans are absent from the stage until the last hundred lines of the second act. They miss Tiberius' testing of Sejanus' political ruthlessness. Having been reassured that his favourite is devoid of scruple, the Emperor and his favourite plot to destroy the Germanicans by picking them off one by one. Sejanus once more soliloquises, and now reveals to us his own ambition to supplant Tiberius. His speech is logical, robust and muscular, physical in its sounds and tropes, but utterly inhumane. Sejanus sees people as physical objects which he manipulates so that he 'will rise' (II, 403):

> This I have made my rule
> To thrust Tiberius into tyranny,
> And make him toil to turn aside those blocks
> Which I, alone, could not remove with safety.
>
> (II, 390–3)

The Germanicans who follow him on to the stage hear news of Drusus' poisoning and that the Senate is sitting. Sabinus, Gallus, Lepidus and Arruntius arrive there first. When their associate, the former general Silius, arrives he discovers that he is to face an accusation from the consul Varro. The transparently bogus case against Silius is spoken by the orator Afer. Having made a robust statement of his services to the state, and expressed a fierce denunciation of the Senate's servility and of Tiberius' tyranny, Silius stabs himself and dies, uttering impeccably Stoic sentiments about the value of

3.1 William Houston as Sejanus, Swan Theatre, Stratford-upon-Avon, 2005. Malcolm Davies Collection © Shakespeare Birthplace Trust.

one's life (III, 330–5). 'Look, is he dead?' (III, 341) enquires the heartless Emperor in a blackly comic moment. The malicious intelligence and ruthless energy of Tiberius and Sejanus render conventional nobility disturbingly comic at this moment.

Next before the inquisition is the historian Cremutius Cordus, accused by informers of praising the republican assassins of Julius Caesar, Brutus and Cassius, in his 'annals' (III, 384). He is of course convicted, and his books are ordered to be burnt. Throughout this scene Arruntius (and occasionally Sabinus) offer a series of comments on the action. Modern editions mark far more of these often sarcastic exclamations as asides or lines to be addressed to just one character than Jonson did in the 1616 Folio.[8] Many of Arruntius' lines seem spoken to himself: 'well worded, and most like an orator' (III, 283); 'excellent Roman!' (III, 286). In Doran's production it was Afer, Silius, Cordus and Varro who addressed the audience directly. Arruntius and Sabinus, placed in an audience aisle in the Swan Theatre, seemed further from audience contact than those involved in the onstage trials. These are choric figures who do not mediate the play for the audience; the play ignores them. Woolland writes that it is Arruntius' meta-theatrical status which ultimately saves him from Tiberius' wrath, as well as his desire not to attract too much attention from Sejanus (who says of Arruntius, 'he only talks' (II, 299)). But Arruntius' observations seem to me to be rarely insightful or witty, contrary to what Woolland suggests (Woolland 2003: 29–30). If we take Jonson's Folio punctuation,[9] many of these interjections are not asides, but heard and ignored by everyone else on stage. Tiberius hears them, but later takes Sejanus' advice that their outspokenness is more likely to make Tiberius' actions seem more reasonable (III, 498–501). Arruntius' aside at Silius' suicide, 'My thought did prompt him to it' (III, 342), is, as Woolland writes, a 'fine example of the play's wry and extraordinarily dark comedy', but is a characteristically pompous and inward-looking speech (Woolland 2003: 30). We are implicated in laughter at the impotence of Roman virtue; we laugh at Arruntius.

Sejanus misjudges his position badly at the end of Act III. He suggests that he should be allowed to marry Livia and thus make himself part of the imperial family. Tiberius does not refuse him, but lets the audience know later that he must now destroy him.

Having resolved to retire to the country for some time, he places Sejanus in charge, but under the observation of Macro, a new character whose third speech is a long soliloquy which reveals him to be even more ruthless than Sejanus.

In the comedies which Jonson wrote after *Sejanus*, a crucial turning point occurs when the protagonist becomes the object of dramatic irony, a condition to which all other characters but him had been subject before. Jonson's best plays have the strange ludic quality of being one vast form of practical joke. The audience cannot but feel allied in knowledge with those characters who are in on the joke. Knowing what we do, we see the play from their point of view. The effect is to make us morally, if not sympathetically implicated in their actions. In the final two acts we now have the perspective of Tiberius and Macro, and the sense of power which that understanding brings us. But Tiberius will not appear on stage again. Ultimate power is offstage. This is not simply a vacuum at the heart of the play. Offstage is not actually Tiberius' hideaway on Capri, but the auditorium and the audience. In the concluding two acts the play's meta-theatricality will be instrumental in the destruction of Sabinus and then Sejanus, and will finally seek to force us to reconsider our own humanity, since we cannot escape implication as members of an audience whose judgement is central to the play's dynamic. As Richard Dutton writes,

> the whole manner of the play is (pardon the anachronism) Brechtian, presenting situations which all centre on the issues of virtue, vice, judgement and action in such a way that the audience must intervene positively with its own judgements in order to make the history live in any real sense.
>
> (Dutton 1978: 192)

Sabinus is the next of the Germanicans to be destroyed. Two spies, Rufus and Opsius, are concealed in his roof space whilst Latiaris provokes him, eventually, to speak openly of his wish for the Emperor's death, at which point they emerge with the words 'treason to Caesar' (IV, 217). In Doran's RSC production the concealment and emergence of Rufus and Opsius was played for laughs, as two men in armour grumbled about having to be crammed into a trap centre stage, and then burst out awkwardly. Doran's insight seems right here. In his edition of the play Ayers quotes speculation about how this scene might have been staged at the Globe (Jonson 1990: 184). But whether the spies suddenly appear by climbing down a rope ladder or pop their heads up from behind the balcony at the rear of the stage, the comedy will arise from the actors' discomfort and the absurdity of the process of hiding. Here our laughter ignores the fate of the noble but hapless Sabinus. We laugh at an estrangement effect which produces a further level of dramatic irony, one which now elides the division between the world-in-the-play (ancient Rome) and the play-in-the-world (the actors in the theatre before a live audience) at the expense of a represented character.[10] The actors playing Rufus and Opsius and ourselves share a joke in the 'play-in-the-world' which, unlike in Brechtian theory, debases our moral and emotional involvement with the 'world-in-the-play'.

In Act IV Arruntius, at his most classically choric, invokes the gods and finds them wanting (IV, 259–76, 336–40). Divine justice has no role in this play, despite the omens which follow foretelling the downfall of Sejanus, as contradictory letters arrive in Rome hinting at the Emperor's intentions towards his favourite. Arruntius is right when he describes the offstage ruler, increasingly like the play itself, 'acting his tragedies with a comic face' (IV, 379).

So far the play's similarities to classical tragedy have been most evident in Jonson's own version of the chorus, and in the fact that important action – Livia's seduction, Drusus' murder, Sejanus' heroic rescue of Tiberius in a collapsed cave (IV, 48–57) – has been mostly offstage. In the final act Jonson deploys the conventions of classical tragedy innovatively and powerfully.

After a grandiloquent soliloquy which echoes Seneca's doomed Atreus (V, 1–24) (Seneca 1966: 84), and a rejection of all deities but the goddess of luck, Fortune (V, 69–93), we see Sejanus take part in a scrupulously historical re-enactment of a Roman religious ritual in honour of that goddess, whose statue he keeps in his house. But the statue 'turns away' and 'averts her face' (V, 185–6). Sejanus is not abashed, but denounces the proceedings as 'juggling' (V, 193) and 'coz'ning ceremonies' (V, 200). Such a supernatural event, all but unparalleled in Jonson's sceptical, materialist *œuvre*, echoes similar minatory portents in classical tragedy, such as that given to the tyrant Creon in Sophocles' *Antigone* or the murderer Atreus in Seneca's *Thyestes* (Sophocles 1984: 111; Seneca 1966: 76). Other omens have already affected Sejanus' statues (V, 26–66). In this play, unlike in Shakespeare, notes Anne Barton, 'such things become not only suspect but incipiently comic' (Barton 1984: 99). But the theatrical impact of this scene is more significant than such conventional allusions. The stage directions (following V, 177) and the ritual pronouncements (V, 171–83) indicate that Jonson required a very detailed historical re-enactment of Roman religious ritual. The strangeness of such an event in a theatrical tradition which paid little heed to such matters – the anachronisms in Shakespeare's *Julius Caesar* (1599) are perhaps the most germane example – would have produced a heightened sense for the audience of the scene's theatricality.[11] Here is a moment where the play-in-the-world is far more present than the world-in-the-play. The movement of the statue makes that sense even more dominant.

In Doran's RSC production the statue moved by some mechanism, to considerable audience amusement in the performance which I saw, so unexpected was this sort of contrivance in such a brutally realistic political play. In the original production, Ayers contends, the statue must have been played by an actor (Jonson 1990: 220–1). Such laying bare of theatrical artifice may well have caused amusement then, too, perhaps in a similar way to the appearance of the bear in Shakespeare's *The Winter's Tale* (III, iii, 58 s.d.).[12] The amusement is compounded when Sejanus describes the statue/actor's contortions as having 'thy neck/ Writhed to thy tail, like a ridiculous cat' (V, 197–8). As in the case of Sabinus, the force which is about to destroy Sejanus is ludicrous to the audience. Yet again, we have a kind of dramatic irony which extends beyond an advantage of audience knowledge and includes a knowledge of how contingent and contrived is the situation in which the onstage Sejanus finds himself in 'reality', seen from the estranged audience perspective at this moment. This position is certainly analogous to that of the absent Tiberius in the plot, but the most important point, I think, is that Jonson establishes a continuum between moral and political judgement on stage and the audience's own responses (see also below, p. 44). It is not that they can make a detached political judgement from the stalls in a Brechtian way at moments like these; it is rather that being a character in the play and being an observer of it is to be part of the same game, part of the same moral enquiry. Overt theatrical contrivance works to destroy Sejanus. As with Sabinus, action which proclaims its play-in-the-worldness intervenes fatally on the characters of the world-in-the-play.

In the first three acts the immunity of the classical chorus from the actions of the protagonist was rudely abrogated. In the fifth act the convention of the messenger's speech is used initially in a similar way. The messenger typically reports offstage deaths of major characters. Here Tiberius' cunningly ambiguous letter which is read aloud to the Senate has the effect of turning them against Sejanus. He is denounced as a traitor by Macro and led off to execution without an exit speech or even a chance to answer the charge. The more conventional use of the messenger speech convention follows, telling of Sejanus' death at the hands of the Roman mob. The speeches of Terentius and the 'Nuntius' (messenger) are the climax and the most powerful moment of the whole play. The last moments of Greek tragedy conventionally feature reports of the pitiful deaths of both the innocent and the guilty, followed by a brief choral epilogue making some moral or religious point. The Greek philosopher Aristotle famously wrote that the 'catastrophe' of the tragedy should 'awaken fear and pity' in the audience: pity for the sufferings of mortals, fear at the power of the gods (Aristotle 1965: 45 (1452a).[13] But Terentius prefaces with these words his unsparing and vivid account of how the mob tore the body of the beheaded Sejanus into such tiny pieces that he has effectively ceased to exist:

> O you whose minds are good,
> And have not forced all mankind from your breasts,
> That yet have so much stock of virtue left
> To pity guilty states, when they are wretched;
> Lend your soft ears to hear, and eyes to weep
> Deeds done by men, beyond the acts of furies.
>
> (V, 743–8)

'Mankind', a sense of common humanity, is what this speech hopes to evoke in the audience, as well as pity for Sejanus. These are the real, indeed historical deeds of men. Events both in this play and in history are nothing to do with classical divinities; they are 'beyond the act of furies'.

Terentius then compares the mob,

> who never yet
> Knew why to love or hate, but only pleased
> T'express their rage of power
>
> (V, 749–51)

to an audience on their way 'To some great sports, or a new theatre' (V, 775). Here Jonson confronts the audience directly with their own complicity – induced through his own meta-theatrical strategies, perhaps his 'new theatre' – in the 'great sport' of this play, where power has been everything, to audience and onstage character alike, and pity and humanity absent. Jonson's catharsis does not demand awe at divine power, but that we show kindness to our fellow humans. The sense of pathos now deepens as the Nuntius brings news of the deaths of Sejanus' young children, strangled by the public executioner. Since Roman law forbade the execution of virgins, his daughter was raped first. In a speech which again echoes Seneca's Thyestes (Seneca 1966: 76) his widow Apicata

> Upbraids the heavens with their partial dooms,
> Defies their tyrannous powers, and demands
> What she and these poor innocents have transgressed,
> That they must suffer such a share in vengeance.
>
> (V, 861–4)

Lepidus, Arruntius and Terentius speak the epilogue (V, 878–93). The power of the preceding messenger speeches to produce pity in the audience emphasises the banality of their conventional sentiments. It is not 'Fortune' that brought about the death of Sejanus and his children, but the cunning of Tiberius and the craven actions of the Senate. In showing no pity for Sejanus' children Arruntius' Stoicism is revealed to be devoid of humanity. Terentius' opinion that Sejanus' blasphemous irreligious views led to retribution from the gods is rendered hollow by Apicata's fierce denunciations of any notion of divine justice. Jonson's great tragedy transforms the genre in a characteristically humanist way, interweaving as it does 'play' and 'reality', making complex intellectual demands and stressing the primacy of humanity in all things. The demands were too much for Jonson's Georgian editor William Gifford. He felt that the play should have ended at V, 743, omitting both messengers' speeches. To Gifford's sensibility what follows is 'merely tedious' (Jonson 1875: 3.146). But he was alert to the complexity of the play which makes it so powerful on the modern stage. He wrote that *Sejanus* 'is, upon the whole, the most involved and puzzling drama, in its internal arrangement, that was ever produced' (Jonson 1875: 3.152).

It seems unlikely that any modern director could breathe much life into *Catiline*. The protagonist is a curiously one-dimensional villain, apparently more motivated by the desire for carnage than power and constantly painted by all, including himself, in the blackest terms. His opponent Cicero, one of Rome's two elected rulers, is a model of good political sense and is praised at length throughout the play. Catiline's plot is exposed by Fulvia, the mistress of the conspirator Curius. Fulvia acts not out of patriotism, but out of pique that another woman conspirator, Sempronia, should have precedence in any 'business' over her (III, 375–9). Cicero denounces Catiline in the Senate in a speech that takes twenty minutes to perform onstage. His fellow conspirators are tricked into incriminating themselves with the help of some Gallic ambassadors and are eventually executed. Catiline's death in battle with government forces is the subject of the Act V messenger's speech. Julius Caesar, the man who would eventually bring the Roman republic to its effective end, is at least a sympathiser with the conspiracy but Cicero refuses to take action against him without proof, diminishing the consul's final triumph in the eyes of its knowing audience.

The scenes with Fulvia and Sempronia have some life and energy, and there are flurries of onstage near-violence (II, 282–4; IV, 491–4; IV, 824–42). There are ominous supernatural effects required twice (I, 311–23; III, 836). Otherwise the play is a static series of long set-piece speeches lacking in colour and rhetorically predictable. Cicero, who dominates the last three acts, speaks in the style Jonson had rejected for the Tacitean in *Sejanus* (see below, p. 62). There is no sustained attempt to include the audience in the drama in the daring manner of *Sejanus* or of the comedies which follow. The opening soliloquies of Sulla's ghost and Catiline (I, 1–72, 73–97) start by addressing Rome, not the audience; one of Cicero's long soliloquies does the same (III, 438–64). Catiline's asides are often clearly directed at himself (e.g. III, 149–53, 155–161, 174–7). Soliloquies are simply planning aloud (Cicero, III, 468–89) or overwritten braggadocio (Catiline III, 714–54).

The chorus, representing the Roman people, speak at the end of Acts I–IV but offer no epilogue. Julie Sanders has argued that the onstage presence of the chorus throughout is a hint of Jonson's broadly republican sympathies: 'the use of the chorus incorporates the role of populace into the play, and, by extension, the audience as well' (Sanders 1998a: 33). But, as Anne Barton has shown, the chorus was 'certainly performed in the theatre by a single actor', making it an unlikely analogue for the crowd who watch. Furthermore, 'unlike most of its ancient prototypes, it avoids association either practical or emotional with any tragic individual or group of individuals. The comments it offers are general, concerned with the well-being of the city' (Barton 1984: 165, 166). It does not offer specific ways of responding to the tragic situation of the play's untragic protagonists and thus involving the audience in a self-conscious process of judgement. The chorus intervene twice otherwise: once, predictably, to praise the righteous Cato (III, 60) and then to applaud the election of Cicero as consul (III, 85). Finally, when Catiline, flouncing out of the Senate, might appear to threaten Cicero, they cry out in warning so implausibly that the play's Yale editors give the line to the other senators (Jonson 1973: 112).

Jonson's preface to the 1611 Quarto expresses his pride in what he has written and his disdain for the audience, who, understandably, lost interest when Cicero takes over the play in Act III ('To the Reader in Ordinary', ll. 5–8). In both Quarto and Folio Jonson declares Catiline to be a 'legitimate poem' in 'these jig-given times' (Ded., ll. 5, 4). How could Jonson fail so profoundly at the height of his powers? R. G. Noyes felt that 'if the tragedy does at moments appear emotionally cold, the reader may enjoy the comfort of realizing that, like a spring, it is also very pure' (Noyes 1935: 316). Jonson attempted to write as pure a classical tragedy as he could, but instead of returning to the best classical source for dramatic writing – Greek literature – as he had with the great comedies he had recently written, he used exclusively Roman models and consequently produced a play to be read, as Noyes states, not to be performed.

CRITICAL APPROACHES

Perhaps because *Sejanus* was unperformed for so long, or perhaps because the play has been erroneously thought of as a historical reconstruction rather than a piece of theatre, recent critics have tended to focus on Jonson's presentation of Roman politics. Julie Sanders's examination of Jonson's politics finds its depiction of absolute power to be a precursor of the effective 'deconsecration' of sovereignty under James I, where politics was to become a matter of court intrigue and the monarch increasingly absent (Sanders 1998a: 23). This is certainly the pattern in the play. The power of the Roman people, who dismember Sejanus in the final act, shows that power cannot be placed in one man. In a play where stage absence carries potency (see above, p. 40) 'the off-stage power of populace action is immense in the context of the play' (Sanders 1998a: 30). She considers that the play suggests that a people deprived of political influence is more unpredictable and dangerous than one whose voice is at least consulted in some kind of republican constitution.

Jonathan Dollimore also found radical political principles in the text, even if it does not recognise its own contradictions. A play whose ending, nominally, celebrates the workings of providence foregrounds, in the actions of Sejanus and Tiberius, 'the demystifying strategies of survival and gain resorted to by those actually holding power' (Dollimore 2003: 138). This contradiction in what the play seems to be saying about human agency makes it, for Ayres, 'a radically flawed masterpiece' (Jonson: 1990: 29). According to Ayres, we are supposed to believe in the 'obviously real and living goddess Fortune' (Jonson 1990: 28), and yet the rest of the play insists that humans are responsible for their own rise and downfall through their own actions. Ayers does recognise, however, that the play is a 'social tragedy' of the Roman people, 'a people fallen from an older, peculiarly Roman virtue' (Jonson 1990: 24). Critics who

have lamented the lack of a conventional individual tragic protagonist have been in error.

The play's examination of the workings of language in the political and moral sphere is of more interest to Lorna Hutson. *Sejanus*
'dramatizes the complex workings of an inhuman political process;
the thrilling and horrible efficiency with which words can be
detached from their point of origin, and reiterated to bring about
their original speaker's destruction' (Jonson 1998a: xxiv). Rumour
gains credibility through repetition in the play, and the power of
Tiberius is enforced through disembodied utterance whose liabil-
ity cannot be traced back to the original speaker, as the letter in
Act V demonstrates. Equally, the words of a Silius can acquire a
meaning quite different from their original intention. Tiberius and
Sejanus have what James Loxley calls 'power explicitly thematized
in language that becomes a power *over* language' (Loxley 2002: 60).
Even the audience are eavesdroppers on accounts of major offstage
events rather than witnesses to those events.

Richard Cave's work has been more focused upon the dramatic
qualities of the tragedy but has always recognised that politics
cannot be separated from Jonson's dramaturgy. 'It is the sordid
reality of power politics as advocated by Machiavelli that is Jonson's
subject,' he writes, 'not, as the theatrical convention would have it,
the seductive glamour' of Shakespeare's Richard III or Marlowe's
Barabas in *The Jew of Malta* (Cave 1991: 35). Sejanus is a character
whose ambition is the near-divine status of emperor, and yet whose
every action exposes the illusory nature of imperial power, to the
point where he becomes 'a comic critique of the original style' of
stage Machiavel, 'a travesty of the type he seeks to emulate' (Cave
1991: 37). Yet there is no moral security for the audience in this
apparent exposure of amoral Machiavellianism. The audience
cannot be sure when the characters of what Cave calls 'the play
within the play that is closely watched by Silius, Arruntius and their
friends' are acting to each other: 'how can we detect the tone of sin-
cerity?' (Cave 1991: 41). This uncertainty of tone produces a fifth
act poised uncomfortably between absurd comedy and savage
horror. All characters are consequently robbed of 'any vestige of
human dignity'. Tiberius is revealed as the true Machiavel, who
'has made all values relative in the interests of absolute rule', which

makes even the audience uncertain how to respond; laughter 'would imply complicity with Tiberius, yet it is difficult to feel tragic sympathy for individuals who are such willing stooges, victims of their own will to power' (Cave 1991: 43). Indeed, Cave has also argued that the play's dramaturgy cunningly makes us view the events of the last two acts 'experientially', as self-consciously we share Tiberius' perspective and our view of the play becomes an 'ethical challenge'. Jonson's dramaturgy denies audiences 'the right to experience theatre as escapist' (Cave 1999: 36).

Anne Barton has a fascinating explanation for the failure of *Catiline* as a tragedy: 'it reveals the extent to which Jonson, by 1611, was temperamentally committed to comedy' (Barton 1984: 166). Jonson could not help breaking with classical decorum by writing the very amusing Fulvia and Sempronia scenes, in creating the comically impetuous and bloodthirsty Cethegus, and even in making Cicero espouse a 'doctrine of expediency and moral relativism' more often found in comic than tragic protagonists (Barton 1984: 161). He was a comic writer despite himself.

In a more sinister vein, Peter Womack reads Jonson's attempt to write English as close as possible to the original classical text as an attempt to produce a self-authenticating discourse, given the authority of Latin in early modern culture. That self-authentication is also the centralising ideology, for Womack, of Jacobean absolutism. Catiline, who fails to argue with the 'burgess' son' (IV, ii, 421) Cicero in the Senate house, is the old feudal warrior caste 'rendered demented and death-obsessed by the universal scope of the Ciceronian discourse' (Womack 1986: 96).

THE PLAY IN PERFORMANCE

The first version of *Sejanus* was hissed off the Globe stage in 1604, after a first performance probably at court in 1603. Though the tragedy seems to have been staged both in Jacobean times and after the Restoration, there is no record of a professional production between 1604 and 1928, when William Poel produced a version on a single Sunday night on an 'Elizabethan'-style thrust stage in London (Jonson 1990: 37–40). In recent years there have been student productions in Britain, including a fine one at the University of Reading in 2002, directed by Brian Woolland. The play was set in the present day, employing the machinery of modern electronic surveillance to represent a world of spies and informers. Characters watched others on CCTV screens and passed comment on their actions. Consequently much of the play's theatrical dynamic was lost, but the final speeches of Terentius and the Nuntius remained powerful and affecting.

Gregory Doran's RSC production of 2005–6 was thus a landmark in the play's history, and certainly influenced the reading of the play offered earlier in this chapter. Originally performed on the bare thrust stage of Stratford's Swan Theatre, costumes were authentically and appropriately Roman. The importance of the legacy of Germanicus in the play was stressed by an opening ritual in which a mourning Agrippina carried the ashes of her dead husband, accompanied by her sons and friends chanting his name. William Houston brilliantly embodied the concentration of power lust which is Sejanus, and communicated his energy and ideas to the audience with great boldness, leaping in the air in delight at his triumphs in the soliloquy which begins the fifth act. Tiberius was the sly, apparently slow-moving Barry Stanton. His soliloquies in the fourth act, where he reveals his plans to destroy Sejanus to the audience (III, 623–9, 648–60), were flashes of theatrical revelation as we realised that all we had seen of him before was a succession of masks, making us both privileged confidants of the imperial power and aware of the vulnerable humanity of Tiberius. During the reading of Tiberius' letter in the final act Doran placed the Emperor and his historical successor Caligula on a balcony at the side of the stage, writing the very letter and, initially, reading it aloud. This did detract a little from the text's sense of power lying offstage in the final two acts, but was visually very effective in bringing out the dramatic irony. The whole production had the energy, pace and relish for language which characterise the best Jonson in performance. Crucially, it also possessed the desire to engage closely with the audience. The play deserves much more frequent revival.

Catiline did hold the stage intermittently between 1668 and 1691. Even with a prologue spoken by Charles II's mistress Nell Gwyn dressed as an Amazon, however, Pepys wrote that it was 'a play of much good sense and words to read, but that do appear the worst upon the stage, I mean the least diverting, that I ever saw any' (cited in Noyes 1935: 303).[14]

NOTES

1. See also Salmon 1991.
2. Anne Barton ascribes the same objective to Jonson and to the character of the historian Cordus in the play (Barton 1984: 102–3). See also Jonson, *Epig.* 95.
3. For a speculative account of Jonson's own political opinions at this time, see Evans 1998.
4. Jonson alludes to *Frogs* at III, 660 (Jonson 1990: 174).
5. For evidence of Jonson's familiarity with Euripides see McPherson 1974: 43–4.
6. For a discussion of this aspect of Greek tragedy with particular reference to Aeschylus' *Oresteia* see Goldhill 1986: 1–32.
7. Houston, according to Paul Taylor in *The Independent* (29 July 2005: 50), was 'truly scary', an 'adventurer for whom power is the ultimate aphrodisiac', as Michael Billington noted in *The Guardian* (28 July 2005: 28). Dominic Cavendish in *the Daily Telegraph* (28 July 2005: 26) wrote of his 'mesmerising muscular assurance'.
8. An accessible modern edition of the Folio text with the original punctuation and spelling is Jonson 1998a.
9. Asides are marked in the Folio with round brackets; see Jonson 1998a: xxxviii.
10. For these terms, see Weimann 2000: 12.
11. For example, the hats worn by the conspirators (II, i, 73) and Brutus' clock (II, i, 191).
12. For a relevant account of that phenomenon see Hardman 1988: 11.
13. Jonson quotes from this work in *Disc.* (l. 2370).
14. The play was indeed widely read in the period up until 1700, with more than double than the number of allusions discovered in this period than the most often cited of Shakespeare's plays (Riggs 1989: 179).

CHAPTER 4

Volpone, or The Fox (1605–6)

In style and form *Volpone* was an innovation on the Jacobean stage and was immediately popular. In this work Jonson created a mode of high-energy, intensely theatrical comedy which sustained both high moral seriousness and rumbustious hilarity.

CONTEXTS

According to gossip in Jacobean London the model for Volpone was the fabulously rich Thomas Sutton, an heirless speculator and usurer who was courted for his legacy by present-bearing suitors (Evans 1994: 54–6). In fact the source of Jonson's comedies was his wide reading of medieval and classical literature. In *Volpone* he draws, for example, from the medieval beast epic of *Reynard the Fox*; from Aesop's fable of the fox who pretends to be dead to catch birds of prey; from Horace's *Satires* (11.5); from the character Eumolpus in the Roman writer Petronius' novel *The Satyricon* (AD 50) (Petronius 1965: 127ff; McPherson 1990: 100–2) and from the stories of the Greek writer Lucian (see above, p. 10).[1]

The influence of Erasmus and Aristophanes is also evident (Barton 1984: 113–14; Kay 1995: 38, 89; Riggs 1989: 135–6). *Volpone* was a new kind of comedy compared with everything that Jonson had written before. This is a comedy which seduces its audience into admiring outrageous fraudsters, and which morally disorientates and challenges from its first scene; but its aim is to educate, by making the audience think hard both about their delight in the play, and about their moral response to its characters and action (see above, pp. 10–12).

Although its comic style and didactic method were a significant innovation in Jonson's dramatic writing, *Volpone* was not generically original. Nearly forty years ago Brian Gibbons included the play in the category which he named 'Jacobean City Comedy', a genre which was very popular on the London stages in the first decade of the seventeenth century (Gibbons: 1968). It was to be this framework which Jonson brilliantly adapted for his own purposes for his next four plays. City Comedies were sharply observed satires, almost always set in a 'realistic' London. The main characters were from the merchant middle class, and trickery and deception were important parts of the plot. There was usually a sub-plot where the action of the main plot was echoed or parodied by characters of a lower social class, and the play ended with marriage; often the chaste and beautiful merchant's daughter married the morally reformed aristocrat. Probably just before he wrote *Volpone* Jonson collaborated with George Chapman and John Marston to write a prime example of the genre, *Eastward Ho!* (1605).

Volpone complies with many of the conventions of this kind of comedy, but daringly subverts the genre in several striking ways. The English tourists, the Would-bes and Peregrine, fulfil the sub-plot function – a place normally taken by characters of lower social status. Most significantly, there is only punishment at the end for all the transgressors. Celia asks for mercy from the judges, only to be brusquely informed that 'you hurt your innocence, suing for the guilty' (V, xii, 106). Uniquely, to my knowledge, an early modern comedy ends in divorce, not marriage (V, xii, 143–4). In the letter which he wrote in 1607 dedicating the Quarto edition to the universities of Oxford and Cambridge, Jonson explains that he deliberately set out to answer those anti-theatrical Puritans who claimed that the stage condoned sinfulness because comedy showed wickedness forgiven, not punished:

> my special aim being to put the snaffle [bit] in their mouths, that cry out, we never punish vice in our interludes [plays] etc.

I took the more liberty; though not without some lines of
example drawn even in the ancients themselves, the goings-
out of whose comedies are not always joyful, but ofttimes the
bawds, the servants, the rivals, yea and the masters are mulcted
[punished].

(ll. 106–11)

In meeting the anti-theatricalists' moral demands, however, he leaves
the audience to ponder why they feel disappointed to see vice punished
in a manner in keeping with poetic justice. Jonson admitted as much
in the dedicatory letter ('my catastrophe [final act] may in the strict
rigour of comic law meet with censure' (ll. 101–2)), but his purpose
remained 'to inform men in the best reason of living' (ll. 100–1).

Gibbons was sure that *Volpone* was a typical City Comedy. He
noted that as the genre developed the playwrights showed an
'increasingly ambivalent attitude towards the skilful, ruthless materialist who knows how to manipulate capital and the technicalities
of the law – and in this sense, of course Jonson's *Volpone* is a
significant comment on the Jacobean background' (Gibbons 1968:
153). Central to this 'background' is the rampant free market in
much of London in the early years of the seventeenth century. It has
been argued by historians that the period from 1580 to 1620 was 'the
real watershed between medieval and modern England' (Stone
1965: 15). It was the period when market capitalism securely established its future dominance in London, at the eventually terminal
expense of the feudal structure of English society. London's
suburbs and old 'liberties', where the theatres stood, were bustling
trading centres of highly competitive commerce and energetic
manufacture. A desire for unscrupulously gained profit seemed to
be everywhere. John Wheeler describes London in 1601 as a place
that recalls the world of Jonson's comedies:

the master with his servants, one friend and acquaintance with
another, the captain with his soldiers, the husband with his
wife, women with and among themselves, and in a word, all
the world choppeth and changeth, runneth and raveth after
marts, markets and merchandising, so that all things come into
commerce, and pass into traffic (in a manner) in all times . . .

yea there are some found so subtle and cunning merchants, that they persuade and induce men to suffer themselves to be bought and sold.

(Wheeler 1931: 6–7)

All things can now be traded; everything, through the operation of money, can be transformed into something else. Nothing is stable and untradable, nothing has value in itself; everything, even a human being, has its price. In a free market economy unlimited self-transformation seemed possible, despite all impediments of birth – providing the money was available to do so.

Contemporary writers also noted that in trading sellers play a role, or put on a show, in order to persuade the buyer to purchase at a price which would yield the seller a profit. At the time John Hall wrote that 'Man in business is but a theatrical person, and in a manner but plays himself' (quoted in Agnew 1986: 97). Making money, self-transformation and playing a role were all connected in the urban Jacobean consciousness. Commercial theatres, purpose-built buildings where the audience had to pay to watch acts of personal transformation, were an important factor in this new consciousness.

Not only are the theatrical skills of Volpone and Mosca expertly deployed to the maximum profit in the play; we also see the delight in self-transformation and performance which cannot be separated from the energy of capitalist accumulation, and which runs through this play like an electric charge. In Volpone's case, the successful deception of the court in Act IV gives him more joy than if he had managed to seduce Celia ('the pleasure of all womankind's not like it' (V, ii, 11)). As for Mosca, his own delight in his ability to 'change a visor swifter than a thought' (III, i, 29) and to 'be here,/ And there, and here, and yonder, all at once' (III, i, 26–7) suggests that his identity has become so many sparking fragments that there is no core individuality to him any more. His soliloquy at the beginning of Act III might be expected to take the audience into his confidence, Iago-like; it reveals nothing but his delight in himself. The amorality and theatricality of the free market are Jonson's subject in *Volpone*; neither stands unambiguously condemned.

The play's setting is not, of course, London, but analogies were often drawn between Venice and Britain's capital, both being maritime trading cities proud of their 'liberty'. Venice was admired in Britain for its ancient political constitution. A republic whose aristocracy elected its Doge and legislative council seemed to combine the best of monarchical and republican politics. Its legal system was famously impartial to all – if severe in its punishments – in order to encourage the foreign commerce on which the city's wealth and magnificence depended (an impartiality which Antonio in *The Merchant of Venice* recognises, and on which his opponent Shylock mistakenly relies) (Shakespeare 1997: III, iii, 26–31; IV, i, 99–103). Yet the Venetians were also notorious for their ruthlessness in business and their political cunning. A Milanese, Canon Casola, wrote that Venetian gentlemen are 'astute and very subtle in their dealings, and whoever has to do business with them must keep his eyes and ears well open' (quoted in McPherson 1990: 35), something of which Sir Pol.'s reading has at least made him aware (IV, i, 12–21). Hutson has suggested that the play brings to the fore the contradictions between political liberty and a just legal system on the one hand and unscrupulous capitalism on the other. The Avocatori's treatment of Mosca in the final scene shows clear prejudice based on a class feeling, whose essence is obviously pure wealth; while apparently a *clarissimo* (wealthy notable) he is to be protected from insult and considered as a future son-in-law. When a mere parasite once more, he is sent to the galleys, not least because he wore the 'habit of a gentleman of Venice,/ Being a fellow of no birth or blood' (V, xii, 111–12). Furthermore, the play's depiction of a civilised and entertaining, yet greed-driven Venetian society draws attention to a new, anti-humanist conception of the relation between individuals and the state, where 'what in an individual was a vice (avarice, social competitiveness) might become, in aggregate, a virtue (national prosperity, civilised manners)' (Jonson 1998a: xxvii-xxix). Julie Sanders has also argued that the *magnifico* Volpone's absolutist rule of his own household is a kind of unmasking of the pretensions of the Venetian republic (Sanders 1998a: 38).

The political 'liberty' of Venice was also thought to go hand in hand with moral licence, especially with regard to luxurious living and sexual morality. The Venetian courtesans, on whom Lady Pol. wishes to model herself (II, i, 26–9), were thought to number between five and ten per cent of the entire population (McPherson

1990: 43). They were famed for their wit and conversation, as much as for their sexual availability. Venetian gentlewomen were glamorously dressed, elaborately made up and coiffured, and famous for their amorous intrigues. The fashion which shocked outsiders was the display of exposed breasts (Lady Pol. wails, as she struggles both to be lady-like and to imitate the locals, that 'this band [collar, neckline] / Shows not my neck enough' (III, iv, 2–3). And yet the English traveller Thomas Coryat, writing in 1611, makes it sound as if Corvino's treatment of Celia (II, v, 47–56) was typical:

> The gentlemen do even coop up their wives always within the walls of their houses . . . So that you shall very seldom see a Venetian gentleman's wife but either at the solemnization of a great marriage, or at the Christening of a Jew or late in the evening rowing a gondola.
>
> (Coryat 2003: 27–8)

The last detail here is intriguing. It suggests a public façade of moral behaviour, combined with a privately acknowledged licence. This would suit the idea of a highly theatricalised society: a quality which made Venice the place where *Volpone*, despite its roots in classical satire and capitalist London, must be set.

THE PLAY

The opening is bold and direct. Leaping from his sumptuous bed, the Venetian aristocrat Volpone blasphemously addresses his heap of treasure as a great deity. It quickly becomes clear, however, that he delights just as much in the sound of his own rhetoric as in the gold itself. Supported by the subtly transparent sycophancy of his 'parasite', Mosca, Volpone explains to the audience how he has no heir to his enormous wealth. By pretending to be ill, he can attract a host of suitors who bring sumptuous presents to increase his hoard still further. He makes it clear from the start that what motivates him is the fun of the deception, not the profit: 'I glory/ More in the cunning purchase of my wealth/ Than in the glad possession' (I, i, 30–2). An opening soliloquy ends with a teasing and sensuous image which sums up Jonson's own dramatic technique, as he makes his audience undergo what Volpone says he makes the 'gulls' suffer:

> Letting the cherry knock against their lips,
> And draw it by their mouths, and back again.
>
> (I, i, 89–90)

The teasing starts immediately. Instead of seeing the deception in action, we are treated to sixty-five lines of lame poetry from Volpone's servants about the transmigration of souls. The dissolution of identity will be an important feature and a central idea in the play, but the three performers are themselves very distinctive: a dwarf, a eunuch and a hermaphrodite. According to Mosca these three are Volpone's bastards 'that he begot on beggars/ Gypsies, and Jews, and Blackamoors when he was drunk' (I, v, 44–5). For some critics these symbolic characters with minimal plot function represent the stunted, infertile and 'monstrous' nature of their father (Barish 1963: 98; Hinchcliffe 1985: 44; Womack 1986: 144). But Castrone and Androgyno might be seen by Volpone differently and interpreted more imaginatively. Castrone might be seen to stand for suffering for the sake of art (a beautiful voice), and perhaps for the libertine's dream of consequence-free sex. Androgyno might represent a sexual ambiguity which can embrace the pleasures of both men and women (I, ii, 54), even if he calls those pleasures 'stale' (I, ii, 55).

The welcome arrival of the first suitor ends their performance. The pompous lawyer Voltore, the deaf and deluded Corbaccio and the paranoid merchant Corvino are each in turn Volpone's visitors. Jonson's dynamic use of dramatic irony is crucial in this first act; it performs the crucial function, in terms of the play's moral strategy, of making the audience amused accessories to the deceits of Volpone and Mosca. It is clear that the 'bed-ridden' Volpone is upstage of Mosca and his visitors for considerable amounts of time and is thus able, both by facial expressions and by use of an aside (I, iv, 17), to make them collude in the deception by sharing the joke at the gulls' expense. Mosca's upstage asides (I, iii, 18; I, iv, 67; I, iv, 124–9) also establish a conspiratorial relationship with the audience, but he nevertheless knows how to exploit Volpone's need to

stay in role as the sick man. There is a certain amount of relish in
the tirade of abuse which he delivers in order to demonstrate to
Corvino that his master cannot hear (I, v, 52–60). The audience can
only watch Volpone's helpless face and wonder if role-playing here,
in the case of a servant, is an opportunity for expressing true feelings, not concealing them. Volpone's own feelings for Mosca seem
to be effusively affectionate (I, ii, 122; I, iii, 78; I, v, 137). Mario di
Gangi has pointed out that a master's erotic feelings towards a
servant in comedy and elsewhere confirmed the servant's subordinate status but at the same time gave the servant a means of disrupting that status, as Mosca does here (Di Gangi 1995: 186–7).
Mosca uses his rhetorical skill rather obviously to make Volpone
lust after Corvino's wife Celia, a woman 'Bright as your gold! And
lovely as your gold!' (I, v, 114). Subtly, power is shifting towards the
parasite.

   Two plot-lines have been set in action by the first act, the disin-
heriting of Corbaccio's son Bonario and the attempt to seduce
Corvino's wife. The first is achieved by playing on Corbaccio's
vanity that he will outlive Volpone, the second by convincing
Corvino that only the presence of some simple young woman in
Volpone's bed will bring about the temporary improvement in his
health which will win rich gratitude. But once more the play's narrative drive is held up, this time by the presentation of two English
tourists, Sir Politic Would-be and Peregrine. In the eighteenth
century the relevance of this sub-plot to the main action was not
discernible to critics, and its farcical tortoise shell dénouement
deplored for lack of taste (Noyes 1935: 88–9). Jonas A. Barish
identified the function of Sir Pol. as a 'comic distortion of Volpone
. . . the would-be politician, the speculator *manqué*, the unsucces-
ful enterpriser'. Volpone on the other hand 'succeeds almost
beyond expectation' in all of these designs (Barish 1963: 94).
Though Barish does not acknowledge this, the sub-plot contrast
provided by the bumbling Sir Pol. can actually make the audience
even more impressed with Volpone's manipulative skill.

   Volpone's extravagant performance as the mountebank Scoto
of Mantua interrogates the nature of rhetoric in the market
place further. That rhetoric was the God-given means by which
the human race was civilised was a well-rehearsed argument in

classical literature.[2] 'A true and genuine rhetoric', wrote one of Jonson's favourite humanist writers, Jean Luis Vives, 'is nothing less than eloquent wisdom, which cannot be separated from wisdom and piety' (Rebhorn 2000: 95–6). Only good rhetoric, it was believed, could be deployed in a good cause. As the provocatively interminable speech develops we see Volpone hilariously losing control of his language in a series of increasingly absurd and protracted similes, especially once Celia has appeared on the balcony above (II, ii, 210–28). Yet Volpone's verbal pyrotechnics entertain; salesmen's rhetoric may be meretricious but it can be fun. Venice is a place where bad language and bad behaviour entertain and engage; the audience are not disappointed when Celia tosses her handkerchief.

Critics who wish to portray Celia as an idealised picture of the pious and obedient wife neglect the significance of handkerchief-tossing to an early modern audience, where the gesture was seen as flirtatious.[3] Her husband Corvino sees her behaviour as casting them both as characters in a *commedia dell'arte* performance (II, iii, 3–9). But, typically, he fantasises aloud about his wife being put on display (III, vii, 100–6) and imagines her being made love to by another man (II, v, 15–20; III, vii, 57–63). As for his threats of violence (II, v, 27–34; III, vii, 95–106), Celia's desire to be a martyr to chastity (III, vii, 24–7) in the style of an early Christian saint or a noble Roman matron (III, vii, 93–4) can come across as a masochistic response to his own voyeuristic sadism (III, vii, 248–56). To Douglas Duncan she is 'pornographically sexy' (Duncan 1979: 158). There is something psychologically deeper and more disturbing about the depiction of this marriage which defies a simple moral judgement. It can eventually leave a feeling in the audience that this conventional classical chastity is re-emerging here as a kind of repressed perverse desire. In any case, Celia's Lucretia-like morality, which regards wrath as a vice more manly than lust (III, vii, 248–9), seems to have no purchase on a world in which, as she herself recognises, everything has its price (III, vii, 136–8).[4] She has not understood the consequences of that development. Ironically she ends the play worth three times as much to a future husband (V, xii, 144) than she was before she married Corvino. As an apparently scarce commodity in Venice, the woman who resists commodification, she has simply become more valuable.

Before we get to the confrontation between Celia and Volpone Jonson has teased his audience again by bringing in the garrulous Lady Would-be instead of the eagerly awaited young wife. Lady Pol. can be seen to be another sub-plot parody of Volpone in that she is obsessed with external appearances just as he is (III, iv, 2–7, 10–12); he is also a character who strives to give convincing performances, often in costume. Like her, Volpone also pours out a great amount of verbiage, often full of pseudo-learned classical and literary references (III, iv, 47–8, 72–6, 87–98, 108–12). It can be argued that the comparison with him makes the audience see behind Volpone's glamour, revealing his true nature as a pretentious, vapid self-deceiver. But rather than being a vehicle for cheap misogyny, Lady Pol. demonstrates that in order to achieve some kind of freedom as a woman in Venice, to be able to come and go as she pleases, to dress as she pleases, and to discourse with men about her reading, she must turn herself into a commodity, available to all. Lady Pol. unsuccessfully propositions three different men in the play (Volpone (III, v, 123), Peregrine (IV, iii, 15–18) and Mosca (V, iii, 40–1)). The model of the courtesan (see above, p. 56) shows that in Venice a kind of female liberation is only available if a woman puts herself on sale. Freedom and the free market are incompatible. What is sad and funny here is that her price is so low. Lady Pol. has turned herself into a kind of automaton, a parody courtesan.

Volpone's attempted seduction of Celia (III, vii, 139–265) is for many critics the point at which the audience's sympathies decisively shift against the character (see, for example, Royston 2003: 6), especially if line 264 ('Yield, or I'll force thee') is played as an attempt to rape her, as it often is (though without any textual warrant that Volpone actually does anything here). Volpone seems more interested in recalling reviews of his past theatrical performances (III, vii, 158–64) and in showing off his singing voice (III, vii, 165–82, 235–8). His sexual fantasies seem to involve a great deal of dressing up (III, vii, 194–8, 220–32), and a loss of individual consciousness (III, vii, 216–18) and identity (III, vii, 233–4) in sensual excess. Peter Womack has pointed out that the fluid transformations which comprise Volpone's erotic prospectus to Celia are an eloquent metaphor for the workings of money itself. Analysing III, vii, 190–8, he shows that:

Lollia Paulina's jewels represent pillaged territories; the diamond Volpone holds represents her jewels; the ear-ring represents the diamond and more . . . The medium of this metaphoric transition is exchange value; one object absorbs another by being able to buy it; this is literally the poetry of commodities. Matter takes on an alchemical fluidity when exposed to the reconstituting power of its pure, universal form: money.

(Womack 1986: 163–4)

Money is the means by which identity is dissolved in the commercial theatre, both inside and outside the world of the play; but in this dissolution there is an erotic charge. Desire is itself theatrical. Jonson's great comedies are sexy, but not in an obvious way. In *Volpone* it is the pleasure of deception through self-transformation which appeals. Market capitalism makes this possible, perhaps unavoidable, but it also transforms the moral foundations of society. His theatre is part of the world, not separate from it, and it is a world in which everything is now in flux. The audience in Tyrone Guthrie's 1964 production in Minneapolis famously applauded the attempted rape (Parker 1978: 35).

But there are moral truths for Jonson, and there will be a language which can express them. In his commonplace book *Discoveries* Jonson noted down a version of Seneca's opinion that 'wheresoever manners and fashions are corrupted, language is. It imitates the public riot' (ll. 965–6).[5] After Bonario has rescued Celia and attempted to have Volpone arraigned for attempted rape, the speeches which Voltore makes to defend the *magnifico* are a marvellous piece of forensic rhetoric (IV, v, 29–92; IV, vi, 31–53). They entertain and delight in their audacious falsehoods and self-conscious theatricality. They are also blatantly in the style of the great Roman orator Cicero (106–43 BC), whom Jonson was to put on stage in *Catiline* (1611) (see above, pp. 45). Jonson favoured the alternative rhetorical style of the historian Tacitus (56–117 BC): unpredictable in its movements, fragmented and elliptical, a style more in keeping with the world of the play and the times in which he lived. It was also associated with scepticism about political autocracy.[6]

Voltore's outrageous overturning of the court case so that the accusers are taken off into custody to await punishment apparently brings the play's action to an end. Eighteenth-century critics found Volpone's behaviour in Act V psychologically implausible (Noyes 1935: 91, 98), but the play does not seek to represent the world in that way. Instead the fifth act repeats the action of the first four acts, producing a sense of closure in the same manner as Renaissance serial music, as Brian Parker observes, 'by increasing the tempo of the final movement, changing key, and, especially, by reversing or exchanging parts' (Jonson 1999: 40). In particular, Mosca and Volpone swap roles, and the pace of action increases rapidly towards the punitive final minutes where we see a performance of sentencing which reminds us of the theatricality of the law courts themselves. James Loxley sums up the dénouement as follows:

> The word of the law is effectively mobilised, the theatre of judgement bearing down on the theatricality of desire; but since this amounts to a theatrical condemnation of theatre it is perhaps understandable that the critics have disputed its justice and sincerity.
>
> (Loxley 2002: 73)

But the sentence does not seem to stick on Volpone; he comes forward to ask for our forgiveness and applause (V, xii, 152–8). Or rather, it is unclear whether this is the actor out of role or the actor in role who asks for our indulgence for unspecified offences. The fluidity of identity so evident in the play now seems to have spread to the distinction between the 'offstage' and 'onstage' worlds; the challenge to our moral thinking, which may possibly have caused offence, is part of the 'real' world, not simply to be confined to the 'imaginary world' of the play, in so far as this play has one at all (see McEvoy 2004: 68).

CRITICAL APPROACHES

The earliest detailed criticism of the play, in Dryden's *Essay on Dramatic Poesy* (1668), focuses on Jonson's moral purpose and the expression of that purpose through the play's structure (see Noyes 1935: 48). These two considerations seem to have remained the concern of modern critics. Some have found a stern moralism expressed through a distrust of all that is theatrical. Others have found that the play's examination of the nature of theatre in the world exhibits a far more ambiguous attitude to conventional morality, one that may be a product of the times and the city in which Jonson lived.

It is the contention of many critics that there is a simple conservative moralism at work in the play, albeit subtly. Edward Partridge takes the play's 'meaning' to have a 'universality'. *Volpone* for Partridge is a condemnation of an unchristian world where men greedily devour one another. Jonson's 'vision' is expressed in a recurring pattern of eating imagery in the play, and in its consistently entertaining and flamboyant inversion of true values: Volpone's use of the language of Christian worship in praise of his gold, for example (I, i, 1–13). In making wickedness preposterous, Jonson taught virtue to his audience (Partridge 1958: 63, 72–7, 111). More recent critics have been uncomfortable with the idea that there are values which stand outside history, unproduced by social, economic and political considerations. Peggy Knapp sees the play as morally conservative, but expressing a historically specific conservatism. For Jonson, 'the old [feudal] way of life (or rather the ideals of it)' had 'the force of moral law', as his poetry and, in particular, 'To Penshurst' (*The Forest*, 2) reveal. A man who is 'nothing but roles' has no shape or place in the divinely ordered universe. Volpone is thus a 'satanic challenger to God's order and society's'. The play condemns a 'world of appearances and disguises' where all the 'old loyalties' cannot be taken for granted any more (Knapp 1991: 166, 164, 168, 169, 170).

Critics who argue for this kind of moralist reading have to account for the insipidness, to say the least, of the 'good' characters, Bonario and Celia. Corvino's wife is praised as 'centred' by Knapp, and as 'immobile' and 'centripetal' by Thomas M. Greene, who argued that there is an underlying coherence in all Jonson's work. For Jonson, the virtuous man or woman possessed the 'centred self': an unchanging, self-knowing, self-authorising individuality in a constantly changing world where men feign their true intentions and feelings, a concept derived, Greene suggests, from Stoic philosophy (Greene 1970: 342). Again, the argument is made from Jonson's poetry and from the masques (Greene 1970: 327–33), not the plays.[7] Celia possesses, says Greene, a 'greater strength' because of 'her own inner centrality'; the play itself demonstrates that a man without a core will be without principle. It is entirely fitting that the final punishments of both Volpone and Mosca should require them to be restrained in one tight place (Greene 1970: 342, 337, 339). Jonson's moral satire amounts to an attack on a debased society which has become fully theatricalised, writes Alvin B. Kernan, and is now incapable of moral reform (Kernan 1973: 10–14).

The view that Jonson's conservative moralism disdained the whole business of the theatre has been influentially argued by Jonas A. Barish. Sir Politic Would-be is the parrot in the beast-fable world of the play, and his function is to be an imitation of Volpone; but in him we see that to pretend to be what one is not is to turn oneself into a beast. Or, rather, that it is 'unnatural for men to imitate beasts. It argues a perversion of their essential humanity' (Barish 1963: 98). Nano, Castrone and Androgyno are mimics and they are monsters, 'half-man, half-brute'; the gender confusion at moments in the play (such as the confusion with Peregrine in Act IV scene ii, and 'the reversed masculine-feminine roles of Sir Pol and Lady Would-be') 'contributes its own kind of abnormality to the deformity of the moral atmosphere chiefly figured by the metamorphosis of beasts into men' (Barish 1963: 99, 101). To act was not only to participate in a debased popular art form, Barish argued later, but to mimic and be inconstant and therefore to betray one's unchanging, real essence. 'The plays show us change as something to be shunned, by presenting us with foolish characters determined to embrace [instability]' (Barish 1981: 145). Jonson's purpose in carefully publishing the Folio of his *Works* in 1616 was to validate his writing in the unchanging, substantial form of print, as distinct from the evanescence of theatrical performance. Yet the plays themselves are fine theatre. Perhaps their very energy and tension reveal a yearning in the writer, considers Barish, for the excitements of a world in flux (Barish 1981: 154).

John Sweeney takes the idea of Jonson's cynicism about the stage further by arguing that in *Volpone* Jonson has abandoned the idea that theatre can be either entertainment or a force for moral reformation; instead it is a species of deception upon the public purely in the interests of making money. The play's very manipulation of its audience, morally and in terms of dramatic expectations, is an expression of the playwright's relationship to his audience; Jonson always remains in control of the meaning of his work (Sweeney 1982). For James Hirsh, the play also demonstrates that theatre cannot reform a foolish world, and that any writer who thinks so is either a fool himself or a kind of 'mountebank selling a phony elixir' (Hirsh 1997: 106).

It is strange, however, that a play which has been the source of so much delight should be considered a condemnation of the arts of the playhouse. Steele, writing in the *Tatler* after seeing a performance at Drury Lane in 1709, thought that 'a man that has been at this, will hardly like any other play during the season' (Noyes 1935: 60); Joan Littlewood, who directed the play in 1953, said that '*Volpone* is the greatest comedy ever written' (Schafer 1999: 160). Perhaps because the play has been performed much more frequently in Britain than in North America, British critics such as Anne Barton and Richard Cave are far less convinced of Jonson's anti-theatricalism.

But it is perhaps an error to suppose that this play is morally or artistically dogmatic. Indeed, as Ian Donaldson has argued, that theatrical delight is produced by a refusal to enlighten the audience of this play about characters' motivations and purposes, and by defeating the audience's conventional expectations:

> Volpone is not just intent upon amassing wealth, or luring Celia into his bed, or achieving any other such clearly definable goal. It is the process, not the end that fascinates him: the infinite and exhilarating play of possibility. Mosca's private purposes may be more sharply defined but to an audience – as to his master – these purposes are still not visible.
>
> (Donaldson 1997: 118)

John Creaser, who considers Jonson's plays to be 'radically elusive', argues that Jonson 'pays us the high compliment of trusting us to be enlightened by uncertainty' (Creaser 1994: 109, 115). *Volpone*, writes Creaser, 'holds two essential orders of value in tense and precarious opposition': the stage, where virtuosity rules, and the world, where moral virtue is supreme. Volpone's epilogue, spoken on an ambiguous boundary between the onstage and offstage worlds, 'leaves us with an insoluble problem made explicit' (Creaser 1994: 110–11). There is a playful but disturbing interrogation of the relationship between life and theatricality throughout. For Peter Womack, the theatrical space has the function of what the Russian theorist Mikhail Bakhtin called 'carnival' in early modern culture: a space where the single voice of authority is challenged by the multiple voices of inversion and parody, where the values of the body come first. Volpone's house is an travesty inversion of the King's court: 'The king wears a nightcap instead of a crown; the courtiers wish him, not long life, but immediate death; the most favoured suitors are chosen for their exceptional avarice and folly; and so on' (Womack 1986: 73). He notes that the early years of James I's rule saw the 'monetarization of the court' which is 'the immediate context for the comic system of [Jonson's] mature comedy' (Womack 1986: 74).

The source of the play's endemic sense of uncertainty has been located in the economic and social circumstances of its moment in history. As long ago as 1937 L. C. Knights argued that Jonson's drama was a blast against the primitive capitalist accumulation which it embodies on stage (Knights 1937). Julie Sanders has argued that 'liminality', the sense of being on a threshold, is a key feature of the play, and that this is a product of the dominance of the values of market capitalism. In the market one thing is transformed into something else through the agency of money. Volpone's bedroom is a liminal space, between the public and the private, the political and the theatrical, like the market itself. Mosca, the parasite, stands on the threshold, both inside and outside the household, and on the dangerous frontiers between classes, genders[8] and moral codes in the play. It is only when Volpone leaves the house that he is defeated – and he then takes refuge on the margin of the stage itself (Sanders 1998a: 41–4).

Lawrence Danson takes this fracturing and lack of centredness to its post-structuralist conclusion. For him, the play exposes the contingency of all social roles and personal identity as marriage and family ties are revealed to be the product of pure self-interest. Volpone, a character with no stable, essential self, ought to seem shallow but he is not. That is because he is 'not just a symbol, but a symbol-using animal, that is a man'. His grotesque parodies of human relationships (with Mosca, with Celia, with his 'children') reveal the 'quasi-miraculous, quasi-monstrous autochthony' of Volpone and of all social identities. He must be punished because 'his crimes expose what society wants hidden, the arbitrary and merely constructed nature of the system of socially organised selves' (Danson 1984: 187, 188). Womack also sees the play as revealing individuality to be the product of social forces, but identifies them as those of the first decade of the seventeenth century, before the idea of the bourgeois individual was fully established. Volpone is funny because he is the pure product of those forces on stage:

> From the workings of that society, Volpone draws not merely (realistically) his income, but his self-enjoyment, his life-blood, his splendour, his false personae of invalid, mountebank, corpse, commandator – in short, his whole existence as a comic character. It's always the laughing mechanism of exploitation that makes up the man, rather than the other way round.
>
> (Womack 1986: 67)

Mosca's success in the play and with the audience is based on the fact that everything he says is for the sake of making money; unlike the others he knows he has no self-determining identity. Only when he adopts the identity of Volpone's heir does he fall (Womack 1986: 72).

The best criticism of the play is always aware of the importance of the experience of seeing this most theatrical of plays in live performance.

THE PLAY IN PERFORMANCE

Thomas Davies, writing in the eighteenth century about contemporary acting, noted how difficult it was to 'personate' Jonson's characters, especially if the 'plays were intermitted for a few years':

> To preserve them required a kind of stage learning, which was traditionally hoarded up. Mosca, in *Volpone*, when he endeavours to work upon the avarice of Corvino, and to induce

him to offer his wife to the pretendedly sick voluptuary, pro-
nounces the word *think*, seven or eight times [II, vi, 59]: there
is a difficulty arises here in pause and difference of sound.

(Noyes 1935: 62–3)[9]

Precise attention to the manner in which Jonson's language is delivered on stage has been the hallmark of all successful productions of
the play since it was rescued from the sentimental condescension of
the romantic and Victorian ages in 1921.[10] The twentieth-century
playwright Peter Barnes noted that despite the difficulty which they
had found at the first reading, as soon as actors

> got on stage with Jonson's lines they found out (a) that Jonson
> knew what he was doing, that he was a pro and he didn't leave
> them floundering and (b) that stage directions were built into the
> speeches. In point of fact they couldn't say certain lines without
> moving. And the tone of voice was built into the speeches.
>
> (Barnes et al. 1972: 9)

John Peter, discussing a weakness in the 1999 RSC production,
insisted that with Jonson's verse 'actor and director have to open it
up almost word by word': if they do this, the play's power is
unleashed.[11] Michael Gambon's successful *Volpone* for the National
Theatre in 1995 had a voice which 'sounds like gunpowder and his
words bang across like bullets'.[12] According to the actor John
Nettles, Matthew Warchus, who directed Gambon, gave the following advice to actors playing Jonson:

> 'Trust the lines; say it on the line; think on the line; use the
> word, not what you feel in your gut and say it immediately and
> don't think about it before you say it'. And this introduces a
> very welcome rapidity of delivery and then the glory of the
> language becomes apparent.
>
> (Cave 1999a: 60)

The great Corvinos have let the language itself form their manic
action, like Jamie Newall in Bill Alexander's 1993 production at
Birmingham Rep. Newall was 'a great flinger of himself, jerking his

head this way, that way, snapping his sentences shut as if they were money boxes'.[13] Leonard Rossiter as Corvino at the Oxford Playhouse in 1966 was

> an effeminate and vulgar dandy . . . pretending with high-pitched laughter that insults are merely jokes, cooing 'Celia I shall grow violent' [sic; III, vii, 93] *sotto voce*, smirking and breathing hard, with his sadism so bottled up that he kept hitting his own body in transports of rage.
>
> (Parker 1978: 158)

'The actor became a tense, twitching battlefield of greed, jealousy and hypocrisy that pulls Corvino apart,' remarked a reviewer (Jensen 1985: 70). As Steele noted in 1709, it is the repression of powerful but unexpressed motivations that makes the work 'prodigious' (Noyes 1935: 59). According to Richard Cave, the actor must 'go for complexities, search for the "delicacies", the anguish or the danger lurking behind the projected public image the character has constructed' (Cave 1999a: 62–3). Productions which use stage business to bring out the characterisation are far less effective. Examples include having two female warders strike Celia and force her to her knees in Act II scene v, as at Stratford, Ontario, in 1971 (Parker 1978: 158), or making Corvino threaten his wife with a hacksaw in the 1991 English Shakespeare Company production; the result is merely 'attention-getting' and, significantly, 'morally null'.[14]

Precise attention to the language in the way indicated by Davies and Barnes will also reveal high energy and careful pacing to be essential to the play's success on stage. Hazlitt, the most sympathetic of Romantic critics, called it 'prolix and improbable, but intense and powerful. It is written *con amore*' (Barish 1972: 49–50). 'The main quality you need as a Jonsonian actor is energy,' wrote Peter Barnes; 'without that you cannot begin' (Barnes 1983: 157). It is possible that Donald Wolfit, who played the Fox in 1938 and then in his own production from 1940 to 1953, 'has some claim to be regarded as the finest' Volpone of the twentieth century (Hinchcliffe 1985: 54–5; see Fig. 4.1). The critic Kenneth Tynan claimed that 'there has never been an actor of greater gusto than Wolfit: he has dynamism, energy, bulk and stature, and he joins

4.1. Donald Wolfit as Volpone, BBC TV 1959. From the Mander and
Mitchenson Theatre Collection.

these together with a sheer relish for resonant words' (Hinchcliffe
1985: 55). Vigorous, energetic and sensual, Wolfit dominated stage,
company and audience; crucially for the success of this role, 'he had
a terrifyingly personal relationship with every member of the audience' (Hinchcliffe 1985: 61). Wolfit's biographer, Ronald Harwood,
quotes the critic John Mayes's account of the 'seduction' scene:

His hypnotic, chuckling laugh as he faced Celia was an extraordinarily powerful moment, and an audience waited, completely controlled, not knowing which way the fox would jump,
and then came the frightening, slow pacing walk towards his
victim followed by another soaring speech of verse splendours.
                                        (Hinchcliffe 1985: 55)

The 1966 Oxford Playhouse production, directed by Frank Hauser,
also had a 'raw power' (Jensen 1985: 70); Leo McKern played the
lead role, according to *The Times*, with 'breathy relish . . . enormous
agility and great vocal skill' (Jensen 1985: 70). The play's energy and
timing have to be very carefully paced, however; Matthew
Warchus's production at the National Theatre in 1995 had, according to Michael Billington, 'just the right intemperate energy'.[15]
Wolfit did his best in his productions to push the character of Mosca
into the background, but Alan Wheatley in the role (Cambridge
1938) superbly controlled the play's 'two tempos' and proved
himself a 'perfect metronome', which helped the extravagant Wolfit
to savour rather than rush the carefully textured lines (Jensen 1985:
59). Productions which get the pace wrong will fail. Despite the
efforts of the director George Devine (Hinchcliffe 1985: 65), Ralph
Richardson's 'over-gentle handling of the main part' (Barish 1972:
231) at Stratford-upon-Avon in 1952, 'drawing out every word to
twice its natural length' (Hinchcliffe 1985: 65), lacked energy and
attack; the play was 'softened and prettified' (Barish 1972: 231). Paul
Scofield at the National Theatre in 1977 spoke (and sang) beautifully, but lacked 'gusto' and took too long to play (Hinchcliffe 1985:
76, 78). Confusing energy and pace for 'knockabout' and turning
the play into a 'romp' is also a mistake. This was the principal
criticism of Tyrone Guthrie's production, which originated in
Minneapolis in 1965 and was played at the National Theatre in
London in 1968. The severity of the final scene rendered all that had
gone before inappropriate, despite Guthrie's impositions on the text
to try to make his production's conclusions work (Jonson 1999: 48).
Leo McKern's 1966 Oxford Playhouse Volpone was considered by
some to be too 'roaring' and 'jovial' (Parker 1978: 155). Richard
Cave observes that the 'exhilaration . . . comes when a production
finds the right momentum' (Cave 1999a: 64).

The director Terry Hands said of Jonson that 'you don't even need to put him on a stage; play him in amongst the house' (Barnes et al. 1972: 17). Since both the moral effect and the theatrical success of the play depend upon the audience responding actively to the play's comedy and requires them to reflect upon their own compromised position within the moral dynamics of performance, good productions go beyond an explicit awareness of *Volpone*'s theatricality and blur the boundaries between the onstage and offstage worlds. Wolfit's delivery of Volpone's epilogue did this in a masterly way:

> Wolfit gathered all the tones and moods together in the epilogue, which he delivered as an actor. The audience could see the man beneath the make-up begging the audience for applause (in one of his [characteristically] hanging-from-the-curtain style postures) but still using the Volpone voice. Thus Volpone's failure in the action of the play became Wolfit's success in the performance of the play: actor and role stood side by side.
>
> (Hinchcliffe 1985: 63)

Wolfit and Gambon both upstaged Mosca furiously while he was in conversation with the gulls in Act I, wriggling comically beneath the bedclothes. Both actors also kept a fine balance between fully feigned sickness and almost giving the game away by snatching the gulls' gifts or by exaggeratedly miming the symptoms attributed to Volpone. The audience were thus made complicit in the plot's deceptions and the play's essential Jonsonian duplicity in the status of the character as performer. Guthrie's Volpones took this even further, kicking away Corbaccio's walking stick and letting Corvino see him examining his jewels (Parker 1978: 168). In the most successful moments on stage, however, it is not the theatricality of the presentation that is stressed but the difficulty of distinguishing between the theatrical and the real. Scofield's 1977 Scoto played the rhetoric successfully as the great verse speaker Paul Scofield as Volpone as a mountebank; Gambon's 1995 Tommy Cooper impression and ad-libbing in the same scene seemed awkward and meretricious. A Mosca who is the audience's close confidant but who then betrays their trust seems to be part of the pattern of successful productions, too. In the 1972 Bristol Old Vic production

Lewis Findlater 'delivered [the soliloquy at III, i, 1–33] intimately to the audience, sitting on the edge of the stage with his legs dangling into the auditorium' (Parker 1978: 161).

Designers who seek to express the text visually generally seem to obscure it. Guthrie's 1968 Old Vic production featured unwieldy costumes which made the gulls look like carrion birds; Anthony Quayle as Richardson's Mosca was dressed in shiny black, rubbed his limbs together and buzzed and hissed like a huge fly (Hinchcliffe 1985: 70, 66); but the play speaks of people and their self-deceptions and performances, not of animals.

NOTES

1. For more detail on sources, see Jonson 1999: 10–18, 309–20. Aesop was a legendary Greek writer of moral tales (c. 500 BC).
2. See Cicero, *De Inventione*, I.2.2–3; Horace, *Ars Poetica* 391–491; Quintilian, *Institutio Oratoria* 2.16.9.
3. Parker (1978: 153) tries to avoid the implication by suggesting that money was often thrown to mountebanks in handkerchiefs. But see Barnes et al. 1972: 11 and Leech 1973: 17.
4. Lucretia (alluded to at III, vii, 100–5), having been raped by Tarquin, killed herself so that the dishonour might be purged. But even in her case her menfolk told her that no guilt should attach to her (Livy, 1.57.58).
5. The reference is to Seneca, *Epistolae*, 114.3.
6. On the Ciceronian, 'Attic', and Tacitean, 'Asiatic', styles see Barish 1960: 48–50; on the significance of Taciteanism see Kay 1995: 69–71; see also Maus 1984: 4–5.
7. For a well-made case that Jonson does not in fact write plays which accord with the views he might express elsewhere, see Maus 1984: pp. 48, 182.
8. For an examination of the homoerotic dynamics of Mosca's relationship with Volpone, see Di Gangi 1995: 186–92 and Barbour 1995: 1006–12.
9. There is a case to be made for the idea that there is only one fully effective way of delivering a line in Jonson which is inscribed into the writing itself. See Potter 1999: 196.

10. From 1776 until 1921 the play was not performed in England. Its characterisation and action were perceived to be 'absurd and improbable', the language 'pedantic . . . and full of Latinity', as well as indecent. See Noyes 1935: 97–8.
11. John Peter in *The Sunday Times*, 28 March 1999; *Culture*, p. 3.
12. Benedict Nightingale in *The Times*, 29 July 1995; WE/5.
13. Jeremy Kingston in *The Times*, 3 June 1993, p. 33.
14. Benedict Nightingale in *The Times*, 7 February 1991.
15. Michael Billington in *The Guardian*, 29 July 1995, p. 26.

CHAPTER 5

Epicoene, or The Silent Woman (1609)

After the great public success of *Volpone* at the Globe Jonson returned to writing for the small private audience at the Whitefriars theatre. The last of the boy companies, the Children of the Queen's Revels, gave their performances there.

CONTEXTS

The fashion for performances by casts of adolescent boys which had reached its height in the last years of Elizabeth's reign was waning by 1609. In this one remaining company the performers were no longer children, 'but young adult players, their leaders aged about twenty' (Gurr 1992: 51); indeed 'there were at least six full adults, some of them with decades of acting behind them' (Gurr 1992: 55). Their audience at the Whitefriars seems to have been dominated by 'gallants', aristocratic young men who enjoyed the satirical depiction of the lives and mores of the middle-class citizens which comprised the theatre's staple repertory. Jonson himself dined with a circle of such witty young men at the Mermaid tavern in Bread Street, a group which included the poet John Donne. W. David Kay has compared the sophisticated wit and sudden reversal of expectation which characterise *Epicoene* with some of Donne's own *Songs and Sonnets* (Kay 1995: 105).

The 'youth' of the company offered an excuse for a scandalous content which the public theatres could not plead. Such a temptation to offend Jonson found hard to refuse.[1] It is possible that a line in *Epicoene* which offended the King's cousin Lady Arabella Stuart may have caused the play to have been suppressed (Riggs 1989: 156). In any case, *Epicoene* does not seem to have been initially successful. Drummond recalled Jonson telling how after its first performance 'there was found verses on the stage against him, concluding that that play was well named *The Silent Woman*: there was never one man to say *plaudite* to [applaud] it' (*Conv.*, ll. 618–19).

Many sources and influences are at work in the creation of *Epicoene*. At the time of its composition Jonson was much engaged with the writing of court masques which celebrated marriage and its joys, and in particular *The Masque of Queens* (1608–9). In *Epicoene*, the conventions of the masque are used to ridicule the play's characters, for at the play's Act III climax the rituals of the wedding masque are parodied and inverted. In the masque mysterious revellers come with compliments for the bride and groom, and the music evokes the harmonious blending of man and woman. In *Epicoene* uninvited guests in the form of four officious, self-important and absurdly dressed middle-aged women enter to complain about the inadequacy of the proceedings and of the welcome they receive (III, vi, 60–92). 'Rough music' is the conclusion of a rising cacophony of noise which ends the wedding party at the play's centre (III, vii, 1–9) (Riggs 1989: 154–5; Donaldson 1970: 37–45). An aristocratic genre is used parodically here as part of the play's overall strategy of mocking the pretensions of its characters, who are aspirant gentry and minor aristocrats on the fringes of the leisured life of the court.

The title *The Silent Woman* addresses directly the feminine ideal of contemporary conduct books. William Whatley in *A Bride-bush: or Direction for Married Persons* (1619) wrote that 'doubtless a simple woman holding her peace shall have more honour than one of more wit, if she be full of tongue'; Richard Brathwaite advised that 'silence in a woman is a moving rhetoric, winning most when in words it wooeth least' (both cited in Luckyj 1993: 35). Female speech is 'scolding', 'shrewish', and such freedom of the tongue used against men was also taken as a sign of a sexually predatory, dominating woman (see Jardine 1983: 121–3). Late medieval and Renaissance folk tales feature the idea of the silent wife as the ideal. In Erasmus's 1528 dialogue *Uxor Mempsigamos* ('The Complaining Wife'), the man who restores speech to his dumb wife is told by the Devil that once a woman has started to speak all the demons in hell cannot stop her (Jardine 1983: 107–8). In *Epicoene*, Morose, a man who hates noise of any kind, seeks out a nearly mute woman to be his wife not out of any desire for a family, but rather so that he can sire an heir to prevent his hated nephew Dauphine getting hold of his property after his death. Once married, his new wife Epicoene reveals herself to be the garrulous shrew he had feared all along (III, iv, 23–47).

Early modern attitudes to the silent woman were in fact ambivalent. Silence could betoken a stubborn defiance or even a sexual availability. Or worse:

> While silence should ensure subjection, a man must have something to go on in his search for a properly submissive wife: a woman who speaks allows herself to be known, hence controlled: by implication, the silent woman, though conventionally supposed chaste, confounds knowledge and hints at the hidden and perhaps even the bestial.
>
> (Luckyj 1993: 41)

Christina Luckyj suggests that Jonson has a misogynistic intent in *Epicoene*: 'while the play thus justifies male anxieties about women, it also pokes fun at men who exalt women's silence but underestimate its subversive potential' (Luckyj 1993: 39). Much modern criticism of the play has presented the comedy as conventional diatribe against women (see below, pp. 85–6). But an argument can be put forward that *Epicoene*'s remarkable manipulation of the conventions for representing gender on the Jacobean stage is a much more subtle treatment of the way female characters appeared in the theatre.

THE PLAY

Epicoene stands apart from the other middle comedies. It is written entirely in prose, like *Bartholomew Fair*, but almost completely

lacks the asides, soliloquies and meta-theatrical tricks which explicitly involve the audience in the great theatrical game so characteristic of that play, and so evident in *Volpone*, *The Alchemist* or *The
Devil is an Ass*. Apart from one soliloquy, those techniques are
lacking right up until *Epicoene*'s closing moments.

As soon as he is married Morose is so appalled by his wife's vol-
ubility that he is determined to divorce her at any cost, and 'lawyers'
are summoned to argue about whether adequate legal grounds can
be established. As part of this process he is even driven to announce
his impotence publicly (V, iv, 38–41). Then forty lines from the end
of the play his hated nephew Dauphine secures for himself in
writing five hundred pounds a year from Morose straight away, and
the rest of the estate at Morose's death – upon the condition that he
secures an immediate divorce for his uncle. Dauphine then pulls off
Epicoene's wig and reveals that 'you have married a boy: a gentleman's son that I have brought up this half year at my great charges'
(V, iv, 174–5).

That a character should be cross-dressed, with his or her original gender revealed as the plot's dénouement, is of course quite
conventional in early modern comedy. But at no point in the play
up until this point has Dauphine even hinted either to any character or to the audience that a deception has been taking place.

I have started this discussion of the play by explaining *Epicoene*'s
last moments because this final *coup de théâtre* transforms the
meaning and tone of all that has gone before. First of all, it changes
what might seem a highly conventional, if not deeply conservative
depiction of female vice into an interrogation of the conventions of
the representation on the Jacobean stage; and further, perhaps, into
the constructed nature of gender in the offstage world. Certainly,
this is not a play whose impact on the audience ends the moment
the applause dies away, but rather one which demands discussion
and comment afterwards.

The performance of gender and its construction are marked as
key concerns in the play's opening moments. The opening stage
direction, '[*Enter*] CLERIMONT. *He comes out making himself
ready*, [*followed by*] BOY' (I, i, 1 s.d.), presents the audience with the
spectacle of one boy transforming himself into a man while another,
who is playing a boy, stands next to him by way of contrast.[2] Their

opening conversation jokes about the Boy's granting of sexual favours to both men and women, and about how women like to dress the Boy in their clothes (I, i, 8–20). Clerimont wants the Boy to sing a song which he has taught him, but another idle young gallant enters: Truewit, a man who passes his time 'between his mistress abroad and his ingle at home' (I, i, 22). The song, which praises women who do not use cosmetics ('th' adulteries of art', I, i, 90), interrupts a discussion between Clerimont and Truewit about whether a 'pieced beauty' (I, i, 75), composed of the products the woman has bought to beautify herself, really is inferior to 'a good dressing', as Truewit claims (I, i, 92). In a play performed by boys, the conventions by which femaleness is constructed in the theatre are foregrounded in a discussion which casually disregards the heterosexual norm. Pleasure and sexual fluidity are also placed side by side here (see below, pp. 87–8).

But having established the subject matter of the drama to follow, the subsequent scenes do not offer a challenging analysis of the construction of gender in their dramatic method. Instead, rhetorical excess and boundless vituperation become the dominant modes of expression. After Clerimont has explained Dauphine's situation with his uncle Morose to Truewit, Dauphine himself enters. Truewit undertakes to do what he can to foil Morose's plans, and the other two then laugh behind the back of the next gallant to appear, Sir Amorous La Foole. La Foole announces that he is to dine that day at Captain Otter's, a man notoriously dominated by his rich wife, a woman whose family were enriched in importing porcelain from China (I, iv, 23). Also present will be the 'Collegians' – Haughty, Centaure and Mavis – women who, according to Truewit:

> live from their husbands and give entertainment to all the Wits and Braveries of the time, as they call 'em, cry down or up what they like or dislike in a brain or a fashion with most masculine, or rather hermaphroditical authority.
>
> (I, i, 67–71)

Thus by the end of Act I there are some ready targets set up for the kind of traditional misogyny familiar from the literary tradition. There is no subtlety in the way the play attacks these targets.

After a very funny introduction to Morose in 'conversation' with his mute servant, a post-horn rudely announces the arrival of Truewit in the old man's house, carrying a hangman's noose; suicide, he explains, is preferable to matrimony, and here is ready means. Or rather, Truewit suggests six different ways for Morose to kill himself (II, ii, 17–28). There follow eighty barely interrupted lines of Truewit ranting against women and their vices, and explicating the perils for a man of entering into marriage (II, ii, 48–129). Morose is not deterred; once he has met and approved of Epicoene, in the play's only soliloquy Morose fantasises vindictively about his nephew's imminent ruin, listing a dozen different indignities which he hopes that poverty will inflict on Dauphine (II, v, 86–114). Two scenes later, when Mistress Otter berates her foolish husband's love of drinking and bear-baiting, she lists the social advantages which he enjoys in marital subjection to her in no less than twelve consecutive sarcastic rhetorical questions (III, i, 26–42).

Karen Newman has suggested one interpretation of *Epicoene*'s frequent employment of the rhetorical figure of *copia*, of which these three scenes are eminent, if not egregious examples (see below, pp. 88–9). But another way of reading these speeches is certainly possible. The *copiae* here are hyperbolic, and that is the source of much of their humour. In *Epicoene* there is no Surly (*Alch.*, II, iii, 69–70, 80–1, 88) or Peregrine (*Volp.*, II, i, 23–4, 25–6, 56–60) to undercut the effects of canting or hyperbolic rhetoric either directly through complicit asides to the audience, or indirectly by deflecting a comment only the audience will appreciate off another uncomprehending character on stage (*Volp.*, II, ii, 92, 109, 159). In *Epicoene* there are no authoritative positions in the 'game' of the play with which the audience are complicit at the expense of other characters. (Consider the positions of Sejanus or Volpone or Subtle in the first four acts, for example.) Morose's soliloquy at the end of Act II scene v is so demented that it invites neither complicity nor sympathy.[3] The rhetoric must deflate itself through its own hyperbolic excess if the play is not to become a one-dimensional savage misogynist rant.

In fact the experience of recent productions would seem to indicate that this self-deflating strategy, of hyperbole slipping into comic bathos, might not be effective. In the absence of those

Jonsonian mechanisms which draw the audience into the game of the play *Epicoene* can fail to achieve this self-aware parody and becomes just brutal and nasty (see below, pp. 92–4). It seems as if Jonson sacrifices playing with the audience in the action of the rest of the play in order to increase the surprise of Epicoene's unmasking.[4] In Jonson it would appear that when the world-in-the-play becomes uncharacteristically detached from the play-in-the-world the drama ceases to delight. What should have the Aristophanic quality of the self-evidently fictional cartoon, 'the game', can shade into naturalism and subsequently seem cruel and sadistic. This could be the problem with *Epicoene*.

Perhaps it is the case that many contemporary actors cannot portray a 'distance' from the script in performance that Jonson's writing requires. The texture of the writing seems in *Epicoene* to require a particular attitude towards the speech on the part of the actor. Jonas A. Barish identified Jonson's meticulous engineering of sound in the different characters' parts in 1960. In Truewit's speech, he demonstrated:

> The rhythm and the sense (if one can so separate them) are asynchronous; where the two halves of an antithetical statement may have rhythmic identity without grammatical parallel, or the other way round; where there occurs, so to speak, an illusion of antithesis rather than the completely realised thing.
>
> (Barish 1960: 149–50)

A example of this is when Truewit urges Morose to celebrate his wedding and not to be so apparently keen to consummate his marriage:

> Would you go to bed so presently, sir, afore noon? A man of your head and hair should owe more to that reverend ceremony, and not mount the marriage-bed like a town bull or a mountain goat, but stay the due season and ascend it then with religion and fear. Those delights are to be steeped in the humour and silence of the night; and give the day to other open pleasures and jollities of feast, of music, or revels of discourse.
>
> (III, v, 36–42)

Morose's speech, on the other hand, is regular and predictable in its balance of sound and syllable. It is 'an affected language drawn largely from books' which possesses a 'singularity of diction and gratuitous floridity' (Barish 1960: 159). The script precisely constructs the actor's performance and possesses the performer in a way which may well be unfamiliar to modern actors trained in Stanislavskian methods. Richard Cave praises Richard McCabe's performance as Truewit in the 1989 RSC production of Epicoene because

> he paced and coloured (one is tempted to write 'orchestrated') the character's vast speeches to show how once ideas possessed Truewit's imagination they took on a manic momentum pursuing their flight through breathtaking verbal arabesques in which he suddenly paused in awed surprise when the rush of words spontaneously evolved an image or perception that challenged his deep-rooted disgust with the world he inhabits.
>
> (Cave 1991: 74)

If the speech is paced correctly, it takes flight itself and adopts a life independent of the actor who speaks the lines,[5] and a gap opens up between the actor and the role. This can have a wonderfully comic effect, too, where the actor's expression and intonation offer a parallel commentary – perhaps apologetic – on the material he or she has to speak. Peter Womack draws a superb analogy with the 'wounded stare' of the late British comedian Frankie Howerd, in this case 'the feeble gesture of a man who is half-aware that he has just said something ridiculous or indecent, and who is trying to outface the dawning realization'. It is a subtle 'negotiation between dramatic and authorial voices' (Womack 1986: 30). Without this evident distinction between the two voices there can be no dialogue between the represented and the real, between the play and the actor/audience, and therefore 'no perception of the extent to which performance and role play permeate all aspects of human exchange' (Cave 1999b: 59).

In consequence the delirious increase in emasculating sound and bustle which invades Morose's house can be read simply as a misogynist association of noise with the vicious woman. La Foole's feast is transferred to Morose's house, where Epicoene has certainly begun to talk. The four Collegiates enter like parody masquers to criticise the proceedings (III, vi), followed by musicians, a crowd of servants carrying food, and then, climactically, Captain Otter accompanied by drums and trumpets (III, vii). Morose is forced to retreat to a cross-beam in the attic, with every night-cap he possesses crammed over his ears (IV, i, 18–23).

Truewit and Clerimont now resume their topic of conversation in the play's opening about what they like in a woman (IV, i, 28–133). A further distancing effect of speeches in Jonson can arise if the audience are aware that the language is a close reworking of a classical source. Thus Truewit's long diatribe against marriage in Act II, scene ii is closely based on Book VI of the Roman satirist Juvenal's *Satires*. In this scene he draws on Ovid's *Ars Amatoria* (Jonson 1979: 171–4).[6] But if the distancing fails, we are left here with the character who seems to be the main source of the play's wit and fun assuring us that rape is what women really want:

> It is to them an acceptable violence, and has oft-times the place of the greatest courtesy. She that might have been forced, and you let her go free without touching, though she then seem to thank you, will ever hate you after.
>
> (IV, i, 75–8)

The unpleasantness continues in Act IV, where the gallants persuade La Foole and the idiotic Sir John Daw that each has insulted the other. Both are cowards and agree to suffer at the hands of the other when blindfolded – observed, of course, by an audience of all the play's women. Dauphine kicks Daw six times ('Daw: What's six kicks to a man who reads Seneca?' (IV, v, 252)) and then tweaks La Foole's nose: 'Oh, Sir John, Sir John! Oh, o-o-o-o-o-Oh-' (IV, v, 294, and a typically precise Jonsonian instruction on the noise to be made). Dauphine's actions only make him attractive in the eyes of the Collegiates (IV, vi, 19–38). In the 1989 RSC production the slapstick element here almost overwhelmed the distaste one reviewer felt ('You may feel queasy afterwards; but the spectacle is irresistible' (*The Times*, 6 July 1989)). But at Manchester in 1980 Dauphine was 'chillingly sincere in his readiness to deprive Daw of an arm [IV, v, 113–14], and lost control . . . in the tweaking of La

Foole, when he had to be dragged back from his screaming victim' (Holdsworth 1980: 59).

Morose is now set up with a 'sufficient Lawyer and learned Divine' (IV, vii, 20) who will find a way of granting a divorce. In fact the two experts are Captain Otter and Cutbeard the barber in disguise. Everything is ready for the play's startling conclusion. In that final moment Jonson sweeps away the audience's security in the prime conventions by which sexual difference was produced on stage. In doing so, he also questions the foundations of the 'naturalness' of what is considered 'normal' gendered behaviour by also brutally foregrounding the strangeness of the convention of the cross-dressed boy actor. As Richard Cave observes:

> If it is an acceptable social practice in particular circumstances for boys to become women to the delight and edification of everyone present, how can we in all integrity make prescriptions about what constitutes a proper normality in gender relations and sexual behaviour?
>
> (Cave 1991: 71)

In this way *Epicoene* makes the same kind of fundamental moral challenge to established ways of thinking which *Volpone* did. It is characteristic of Jonson that the impact is produced by turning the whole play into what is effectively a hilarious practical joke played at the audience's expense, and at the same time violently jarring meta-theatre.

But if everything is gambled on one brilliant moment, does that masterstroke make up for the apparent revelling in cruelty, mistrust and hatred which some critics have taken to characterise most of this play's action and dialogue?

CRITICAL APPROACHES

It is not surprising therefore that *Epicoene* has been read as a prime instance of Jonsonian anti-feminism. Mary Beth Rose has claimed that 'in all of Jacobean drama, no misogyny is so detailed and unmitigated, so utterly triumphant, as Ben Jonson's is in *Epicoene*' (Rose 1988: 57). For Rose, anti-feminism goes hand in hand with a conservative opposition to the rise of a new bourgeois social class. The City Comedy genre (see above, p. 53) constitutes a satirical examination of this link between urban social mobility and the struggle for female independence and equality. The focus here is on a transvestite title figure used to defend established social status from a newly created upstart knight.

Rose sees all the characters of the play to be marginal to the aristocracy and struggling to achieve, exploit or retain that identity. Truewit strives to achieve the income from his uncle which would ensure a leisured lifestyle, whilst the former courtier Morose (III, iv, 26–7), jealous of his nephew's knighthood (II, v, 99–104), schemes to deny him that inheritance. La Foole's dubious Irish knighthood[7] gilds a social ineptness (I, iii, 27–37) which he attempts to excuse with irresponsible extravagance (I, iv, 49–57). But if the 'male fools are contemptible . . . the women are beneath contempt' (Rose 1988: 56) in their trivial status games and slanders. They squabble over precedence (III, vii, 31–5) and scheme against one another in an attempt to seduce Dauphine (V, ii, 1–37). Not that any adultery takes place: Rose argues that the actions of the Collegiates, with their cultural and intellectual pretensions, 'suggest not the dangerous temptations of eros, but the drive towards female equality and independence, which Jonson depicts as an aggressive attempt to usurp male authority' (Rose 1988: 57).

The play's conclusion reinforces Jonson's misogyny in its manipulation of the conventional ending of romantic and City Comedy, writes Rose. There is no marriage, but in fact a declaration of impotence with the intention of undoing a marriage. In romantic comedies the ambiguous and exploratory androgyny of a Viola (*Twelfth Night*) or a Rosalind (*As You Like It*) is contained by the play's closure as the heroine is absorbed into the patriarchal institution of marriage. But here 'Epicoene's female disguise dramatizes no ambiguity, contains no complexity: as it turns out, the only possible silent woman – the best woman – is, simply a man' (Rose 1988: 59). In the misogynistic fantasy world of *Epicoene* Truewit does not achieve wealth through marriage. Troublesome sexual desire for women is not needed to 'guarantee the perpetuation of society, but acquisition, secrecy and wit, all exercised in the service of preserving traditional rank and hierarchy' (Rose 1988: 63).

Other critics, such as Richmond Barbour, have been more ambivalent about the sexual politics of the play, recognising that 'Jonson is deeply divided, by turns authoritarian and subversive' (Barbour 1995: 1006). As Barbour recognises, Rose ignores the significance of the epicene youth on the Jacobean stage, especially in a play originally written for a boys' company. The boy actor on the Jacobean stage, he suggests, offered a show in which 'men and women might find mutual pleasure' (Barbour 1995: 1014) as a contrast to the gender enmities elsewhere so prevalent, especially in this play. In his own *English Grammar* (1640) Jonson defines 'epicene' as a category which 'understands both kinds: especially when we cannot make the difference' (HSS VIII: 507). Barbour points out that:

> everyone in the play is drawn to the young Epicoene. S/he is
> the charming common term circulating among all the charac-
> ters. Truewit flirts with her; Daw and La Foole follow her;
> Morose marries her; the Ladies invite her into their college; in
> the end Dauphine claims him, at least for the time being.
>
> (Barbour 1995: 1016)

In the same way the boy actor on the stage, dressed as a socially or sexually ambitious woman, allowed men to feel relatively unthreatened by the representation of women taking on male functions, and permitted women to admire tacitly a representation of a more powerful self which society proscribed. For both men and women the mutual attraction of the youth's body was 'central to forging an erotic community' in the theatre. In the play itself desire for youths seems evident among both sexes. In the first scene Clerimont's boy servant talks of being both 'the welcom'st thing under a man' (I, i, 8–9) and the object of women's desire: a desire that wants to find expression in cross-dressing him (I, i, 12–20). It is not commented on that Clerimont himself has an 'ingle', or catamite (I, i, 22) (see above, p. 80). The work of Lisa Jardine (1983: 9–33) and Stephen Orgel (1996: 35–49) has argued convincingly that homoerotic pleasure at the spectacle of cross-dressed youths, coexisting with heterosexual desire, was clearly an element of the attractions of the early modern stage for many men.[8] The play's dénouement, when Epicoene is revealed as 'spectacularly male', argues Barbour, 'does not erase the boy's promiscuous appeal: the revelation forces the audience to recognise it' (Barbour 1995: 1017). The play in its original production was not so much a savage blow struck in the sex war as the foregrounding of a common desire between men and women which enables some kind of truce to take place and everyone to enjoy the social satire; 'despite some nervousness, the play manages to laugh not at, but with the women' (Barbour 1995: 1015).

Like Rose, Jean E. Howard has censured the play's misogyny whilst also noting that *Epicoene* does accommodate the presence of women spectators, even if only to allow the aristocratic female audience at the Whitefriars to look down on the vulgarity of the Collegians and Mrs Otter and to define their femininity 'against that of their "unnatural"' social inferiors (Howard 1994: 109). Karen Newman has observed how middle-class women in the play become the trope of those 'urban vices', and in particular consumerism, which are a threat to the traditional values of the landed elite. Captain Otter's overheard 'blazon' of his wife identifies her as both consumer and commodity:

> OTTER
> A most vile face! And yet she spends me forty pounds a year
> in mercury and hogs' bones. All her teeth were made i' the
> Blackfriars, both her eyebrows i' the Strand, and her hair in
> Silver Street. Every part o' the town owns a piece of her.
> MISTRESS OTTER
> I cannot hold.
> OTTER
> She takes herself asunder still when she goes to bed, into
> some twenty boxes, and about next day noon is put together
> again, like a great German clock.
>
> (IV, ii, 80–7)

Furthermore, in a play about a woman who will not hold her tongue, consumerism is figured as female, and allied to the expenditure of words as much as money: 'the talking woman represents the city *and* what in large part motivated the growth of the city – mercantilism and colonial expansion. Consumption, like female talk, is presented as at once stereotypical (women all do it) and unnatural (women who do it are masculine, hermaphroditical, monstrous)' (Newman 1989: 509).

Newman further notes Jonson's fondness in the play for the rhetorical figure of *copia*, where a long list of qualities or attributes is ascribed to something (see above, p. 81), often ending with a suggestion to the listener to supply the rest of the series themselves, such as Otter's blazon or the whole series of *copiae* in Truewit's misogynistic diatribe (II, ii, 48–129; see above, p. 81). Ingeniously, Newman suggests that the series of terms in a *copia* represents the abundance of consumerism, but the way in which the list ends leaves the listener with a sense of incompleteness, of a desire for more; and woman is figured as a 'lack', both in the early modern idea of woman as unfinished man and in the psychoanalytical sense. Thus even the play's characteristic rhetorical figure identifies consumption with women: 'the relations of all women to commodification are represented as the same, which tends to level class difference' (Newman 1989: 512).

Marjorie Swann has taken an examination of how the play deals with women, class and commodification further. Dauphine's victory over Morose is a statement of the power of the new capitalist values of the city (see above, pp. 54–5) inasmuch as the nephew's 'economic activism [in employing the boy as Epicoene] mocks the reproductive basis of patrilineage' because he becomes Morose's heir by contract, not by human reproduction; yet even as he does so he acquires an income which is suitable to his status as a knight, and thus 'it allows him to buttress his position within the hereditary social order' (Swann 1998: 298). Dauphine's act throws into question the role of women and marriage in such a situation. If chaste wives are no longer the essential element required for the legitimate transfer of property between generations, then women are empowered in new ways. And, indeed, at the end of the play the women remain unpunished, unlike Daw, La Foole and Morose who are disgraced publicly. The Collegiates will continue to behave promiscuously, and are not reabsorbed into male authority as usually happens at the end of a comedy. They have been duped by Dauphine, but so has the audience:[9] 'the Collegiates are not harshly censured because their traditionally monstrous behaviour has become socially insignificant' (Swann 1998: 302–3).

Where Newman identified women in the play with consumption, Swann sees them as both consumers and consumed. Swann reads Captain Otter's account of his wife's components (IV, ii, 80–9; see above, p. 88) as a rewriting of the 'Petrarchan blazon in commercial terms. The collection of precious metals which denotes female beauty in traditional amatory verse now becomes a list of items purchased by Mistress Otter in the marketplace' (Swann 1998: 306–7). Moreover, that market place, the city, is under the control of male manufacturers: 'Every part o' the town owns a piece of her' (IV, ii, 83). In Mistress Otter's dream, it is the city itself that keeps her social aspirations in check (III, ii, 60–70). Husbands are not needed to keep women in control, as the existence of the Collegiates demonstrates. Women, as consumers and consumed, are subjugated by the market and its commodity relations. They cannot possess autonomous identities, but are 'pieced' together, like Mistress Otter.

Swann concludes that the play is both conservative and radical at the same time in its depiction of social process in proto-capitalist Jacobean London. It shows how capitalism reforms the nature of class and gender superiority whilst making no real change to those in power: aristocrats like Dauphine and men in general. And yet at same time the play offers the radical insight that class and gender distinctions in the play are constructed. Jonson can also be seen to recognise that:

> through consumerism, women gain agency as they use their bodies to fabricate their own identities. Ironically . . . Jonson presents a vision of how women could, like Dauphine, be emancipated by commercial capitalism in the very process of representing such a vision as unthinkable.
>
> (Swann 1998: 311–12)

Jonson himself was, after all, a professional writer selling his work in a market place and thereby gaining social status; yet plays such as *Epicoene* satirise, from a conservative viewpoint, the very economic relations which provide him with both his identity and status.[10] Furthermore, the actor who played Epicoene, Nathan Field, had been schooled by Jonson himself and performed in three of his plays. As Swann observes: 'thus the mercenary alliance between Dauphine and his boy-actor parallels the relationship between the dramatist and actor who collaborated in presenting *Epicoene* at the Whitefriars' (Swann 1998: 313 n. 17).

THE PLAY IN PERFORMANCE

Even if the shock of the original production can never be repeated, if the play's examination of the representation of gender is to work a young, all-male cast would seem to be necessary. After the Restoration the part of Epicoene was played by Edward Kynaston, initially with no women in the company. For the watching diarist Samuel Pepys, Kynaston was 'clearly the prettiest woman in the whole house' (quoted in Noyes 1935: 177). But from 1663 until the eve of the play's disappearance from the London repertory in 1776[11] the role was taken by a woman in mixed cast. In doing so the whole purpose of the play's representational strategy and the dramatic impact of the dénouement are clearly lost. William Poel, having watched an all-male cast of Cambridge undergraduates revive the play in 1909, pointed out that:

> if one of the female parts is played by a male, while the others are in hands of females, it must be very difficult for the audience not to see the difference, and not know all through that Epicoene is really a boy. Once that feeling is allowed to enter, the point of the joke is lost.
>
> (*The Times*, 22 February 1909; HSS IX: 220)

Very few of the infrequent twentieth-century productions of *Epicoene* have repeated the Cambridge casting.[12] The programme of Laurence Boswell's 1980 production in Manchester revealed the sex of the actor in the role from the start (Holdsworth 1980: 58). The 1959 Margate Stage Company cast as Epicoene, according to Ian Donaldson, 'a nicely-rounded girl with shoulder-length hair' (quoted in Jensen 1985: 34).[13] More cunningly, the programme for the 1989 RSC revival ascribed the role to Hannah John, but it was soon fairly clear to the audience that the part was in fact played by John Hannah.

At the Theatre Royal York in 1984 Epicoene was played by a young man, even if the programme claimed that the role was taken by 'Katy Rigley' (Holdsworth 1984: 131). When Dauphine pulled off Epicoene's wig 'the actor's appearance remained totally unchanged, since his own locks were of an identical length, colour and texture with the wig' (Cave 1991: 73). Cave recalls the moment as 'a bold invention with some of the sexual charge of Jonson's conceit' (Cave 1991: 73), but because the gesture was irrelevant to the current conventions by which gender is performed on stage, its impact can have been nothing like the shock of the moment in 1609. None of these relatively recent productions can ever reproduce the effect Jonson seems to have striven for; perhaps it is impossible to do so today at all.

John Hale, the director of the Bristol Old Vic production of 1959, took the view that 'in *Epicoene* Jonson put aside his "high and moral purpose" and "set out with the sole object of making the audience laugh"' (Jensen 1985: 30). If a modern production cannot, through acting which is receptive to Jonson's text, open up a critical distance between script and performer (see above, p. 83), it is plausible that a successful production might sweep the audience along with its energy, noise and vitality and only at the end leave them pondering their complicity in Dauphine's disproportionate vengeance against his misanthropic but not entirely malevolent uncle, not to mention the merely idiotic La Foole and Sir John Daw.

This seems to be largely the case with the 1989 RSC production directed by Danny Boyle (see Fig. 5.1). Irving Wardle in *The Times* (6 July 1989) acknowledged 'the brutality of the plot', and called it 'a production of rampant virility and grotesque comedy, with no appeals for sympathy whatever'. The gallants were 'Jacobean louts . . . every homosexual or androgynous reference was picked up, but seemed no more attractive than the predatory heterosexuality of the Collegiates' (Jonson 2003: 87) The humiliations of the final scene 'are dispatched with blood-sport gusto'. There were literally no punches pulled. Dauphine's cruel final lines to his uncle were accompanied by a slap across the face with the very papers which Morose had just signed: 'Now you may go in and rest, be as private as you will sir. I'll not trouble you till you come to trouble me with your funeral, which I care not how

5.1 David Bradley as Morose and Richard McCabe as Truewit
in *Epicoene*, Swan Theatre, 1989. Joe Cocks Studio Collection ©
Shakespeare Birthplace Trust.

soon it come [*Exit Morose*]' (V, iv, 199–201). As Lois Potter
reports:

> Depending on the performance, the audience either gasped or
> reacted with stunned silence. Jonson might have approved:
> after all, Truewit's final request for applause [V, iv, 235–7]
> makes sure the spectators remember how much agony Morose
> has already suffered from just the kind of noise they are being
> asked to make . . . an automatic symbol of closure was turned
> into a potentially difficult moral choice.
>
> (Potter 1999: 202)

According to Wardle, once the initially confusing 'energy and
speed' of the opening scenes settled down, the performance 'relaxes
into a sure stride' and the play builds to 'a delirious climax'. In

the 1909 Cambridge production Poel had recognised the crucial importance of rising pace and energy in sweeping the audience forward. It is 'a steady crescendo rising through four acts from Truewit's post-horn' (II, ii) onwards; 'it is – or should be – a cause of continuous and ever growing laughter' (quoted in Jensen 1985: 35). The *Observer* review of the 1924 London production by the Phoenix Society described it as 'a sort of literary Niagara in full spate' (quoted in Jensen 1985: 32). The play's pattern of rising sound and energy leads to the shock of the final lines and forces the audience to confront their own acquiescence in the bullying of Morose and the others, and to examine how well justified their laughter was.

The alternative is to see the nastiness of the play emerge at face value, intentionally or otherwise. Two productions in the 1980s went out of their way to create sympathy for Morose. Laurence Boswell in Manchester in 1980 turned the gallants into 'sneering dandified idlers' who 'were cruel and nasty in their treatment of the dupes, but portrayed a curiously parasitic dependence upon them'. Dauphine was 'tall, languid and icily remote' and enjoyed hurting Daw and La Foole (see above, p. 84; Holdsworth 1980: 59). The noises used to torment Morose were so loud that the audience were made to suffer sympathetically with him. Overall, the play was, it seems, too noisy and clamorous, and overdid the violence at any opportunity. At York in 1984 the gallants were 'boisterously coarse' punks, while 'everyone else (except, curiously, Morose) was grotesquely foolish'. Morose, who had 'qualities of candour and dignity in a world peopled by sadistic lunatics', seemed 'to fall quite sincerely in love with' Epicoene, and quietly wept for joy when introduced to her. As at Manchester, 'the air of headlong frenzy' was also overdone in this production, with the result that 'all sense of the play's subtler rhythms of action, as well as much of its verbal and dramatic wit, were buried in the rush' (Holdsworth 1984: 130–1). The evidence of these two productions would suggest that getting the play's pace and energy levels right and achieving its full moral impact may well go together; in Jonson the physical and the moral, the pleasure and the profit, cannot be separated.

NOTES

1. Drummond was of the opinion that Jonson was 'given rather to lose a friend than a jest' (Conv., l. 605).
2. If, indeed, a boy did play Clerimont; see above, p. 76.
3. The productions at Manchester (1980) and York (1984) both cut this speech and thus increased the sympathy of the audience towards Morose (Holdsworth 1984: 131).
4. This does not apply in a modern production where the audience knows that Epicoene is played by a man, and so consequently will probably have guessed the nature of Dauphine's deception straight away. Consequently the audience remain 'superior to the stage-world throughout' (Cave 1991: 73).
5. The actor John Nettles has compared the experience of speaking Jonson's language well to being carried along on a surfboard (Cave 1999b: 60).
6. For an account which identifies the play's hostility to women and the effeminisation of men as a trope for Jonson's ambivalent 'anti-theatricalism' see Levine 1994: 73–88. As with Womack (see below, p. 144), Levine insists in her argument on an unwarranted conflation of deception with theatricality.
7. 'In 1599, during his Irish campaign, the Earl of Essex had been sharply criticised for cheapening the title by bestowing it too liberally' (Jonson 1979: 29).
8. See also the discussion in Howard 1994: 110ff.
9. Swann cites Millard 1984: 155 in support of this particular point.
10. See Wayne 1982: 107.
11. At that time in a considerably altered version by George Colman (Noyes 1935: 208–19).
12. There was, intriguingly, an all-female student production at Birkbeck College London in May 1911 (HSS IX: 221).
13. The rather reactionary intention of this updated production seemed to be to 'exploit . . . the present day difficulty of telling the boys from the girls' (Jensen 1985: 34).

CHAPTER 6

The Alchemist (1610)

A fter *Epicoene*, Jonson returned to work for the King's Men at their new indoor playhouse at Blackfriars. His ingenious new play, *The Alchemist*, played boldly with time and space. Jonson's great twentieth-century editors saw it as 'the most signal triumph of Jonson's difficult and original dramatic art' (HSS II: 88).

CONTEXTS

The action of the play takes place inside and directly outside Lovewit's house in Blackfriars: 'here, in the Friars' (I, i, 17). There seems to be general agreement that the play was first performed at the Blackfriars Theatre.[1] The Blackfriars was a former monastic refectory which had been leased by the King's Men as an indoor playhouse since 1608. Entrance cost more than the 'public' playhouses, and it seems to have attracted a more elite and less socially mixed audience (Gurr 2004: 31).

Its location was significant. The Blackfriars 'liberty', standing as it did on former church land, had been free from the control of the Mayor and Corporation. The London liberties were the most unregulated and commercially vibrant parts of the city until their absorption into the City's sphere of authority in 1608. Artificers and tradesmen flocked to these suburbs to manufacture and to trade outside the reach of the old guilds. In the Blackfriars liberty the theatre stood on the same site as a glassworks. James Burbage, who converted the old frater into a 'hall' theatre, was avoiding the more controlled wards of the city with the same intentions as those who ran the brothels of Southwark or who traded in the markets of Spitalfields.[2]

Face, Subtle and Dol are performers and tradesmen themselves, in an extremely free market. 'Captain Face' is Lovewit's butler, Jeremy, who is looking after the house while his master is out of London to avoid the plague, which had seriously affected London in the summer of 1610 (HSS IX: 224). His accomplices are Subtle, the 'alchemist', and Dol Common, a prostitute who is as accomplished a performer as the other two. They set themselves up as a joint-stock company, a 'venture tripartite' (I, i, 135), to fleece the inhabitants of Blackfriars. Face does the marketing, bringing clients to the house who hope to profit from Subtle's imminent achievement of the 'philosopher's stone'. Their customers offer various down payments on their desired purchase. Dol (public relations) plays whatever role is needed to keep up the illusion – a mad lord's daughter, or the Queen of Fairy.

In *The Alchemist* Jonson explores the connections between deceit, rhetoric, theatrical pretence, money-making and the human desire to be more than what we currently are. Remarkably, those connections are constituted by the physical location of the theatre itself and the immediate moment of the play's performance. Blackfriars was a dynamic, 'marginal' area of London in sociological transition (Sanders 1998a: 68–9). The play stands on the margin of the city, criticising London's mores and habits. But it is marginal in another sense, since it also thrives on the transitions between the offstage and onstage worlds and the continuum between them. It stands in the margins of both 'worlds' at once. The play's immediacy, its merging of the world inside the play and the 'real' world around it, its unmediated display, is perhaps its most brilliant feature.

Unlike many of his intellectually respectable contemporaries, Jonson's attitude to alchemy is entirely sceptical. The belief that 'base' metals could be transformed into gold, and that gold in turn could be elevated into 'the philosopher's stone' was an ancient one, and the knowledge of the process was supposed to be contained in various hermetic and cabbalistic texts from past ages.[3] Alchemy had its own dense and impenetrable jargon (see, for example, II, iii, 143–98), and offered a marvellous opportunity for satire and mischief-making. One of Jonson's *Epigrams* (VI) scorned the hypocrisy of the alchemists, and his 1616 masque *Mercury Vindicated From the Alchemists at Court* ridiculed their pretensions as they sought to improve on nature. According to Drummond, Jonson could not resist mocking occult beliefs even outside the theatre:

> He, with the consent of a friend, cozened a lady with whom he had made an appointment to meet an old astrologer in the suburbs, which she kept: and it was himself disguised in a long gown and a white beard at the light of [a] dim-burning candle, up in a little cabinet reached unto by a ladder.
>
> (*Conv.*, ll. 254–8)

Alchemists were supposed to be motivated not by greed for gold, but by piety (II, ii, 97–100). The philosopher's stone, their ultimate goal, was the perfect, indestructible quintessence of all the elements. It was a blessed, sacred thing which contained the divine spirit itself, it was claimed (Ellis 2005: 27). It would guarantee immortality and restore to the ageing body its perfect, youthful condition (see Mammon's prediction at II, i, 63–70) (Ellis 2005: 27). Thus alchemy was ultimately a process for stopping time itself, as well as for bringing about the final utopian state: a restoration for humanity of the conditions of the Garden of Eden, albeit perhaps in apocalyptic conditions.

The Alchemist not only is most explicit in its reference to the passing of the hours, but is also Jonson's most scrupulously time-bound play (see below, pp. 101–2). The coiled tension in the comedy is the product of its strict time-scheme, overtly counting down the ageing of the world and of its characters who yearn, vainly, for an escape from history altogether. Sir Epicure Mammon, who dreams of a 'fifth monarchy' (IV, v, 34), wishes to use the stone to bring about a utopia; the Anabaptists Ananias and Tribulation plan to establish the rule on earth of God's chosen 'saints'. In such a meta-theatrical play as this, which constantly foregrounds its own materiality as a process in the real world, the impossibility of

escaping history is powerfully juxtaposed with the delight of an art-
form (theatre, not alchemy) that hints at the possibility of just such
an escape in the strange 'otherness' of the moment of theatrical creation. Theatre is genuine alchemy, and the play, despite itself, celebrates this fact.

THE PLAY

The Alchemist famously offers one of the most striking openings of
any English play: '*Face*. Believe't, I will. *Subtle*. Thy worst. I fart at
thee' (I, i, 1). Noxious fumes and vapours are going to feature
heavily in this play as an analogy for the fog of jargon and verbiage
which constitutes much of the text: a fog which is itself a reflection
of the shifting murkiness of the personal identities of the venture
tripartite. Furthermore, Jonson demonstrates how money, the most
protean of all substances, creates individual identity in the world of
the play.

As Peter Womack points out, an important feature of Jonson's
dramatic verse is the way that it piles up term after term, saying
one thing and saying it again, producing great lists of verbiage.
The language 'supplements', he says, to the point where its
meaning 'disintegrates' (Womack 1986: 3). The language gratu-
itously offers more than one way of saying the same thing until the
unresolved heterogeneity of objects is constantly threatening to
subvert the intentional unity proposed by the syntax (Womack
1986: 4), as can be seen when Face describes how he has set Subtle
up in business:

> *Face*. When all your alchemy and your algebra,
> Your minerals, vegetals, and animals,
> Your conjuring, cozening, and your dozen of trades,
> Could not relieve your corpse, with so much linen
> Would make you tinder, but to see a fire;
> I ga' you countenance, credit for your coals,
> Your stills, your glasses, your materials;
> Built you a furnace, drew you customers.
>
> (I, i, 38–45)

Furthermore, Womack later argues that the self-conscious and overwhelming use of rhetorical figures in Jonson's great set-piece speeches and dialogues directs language away from referentiality to the point where it becomes a kind of cant or 'linguistic junk' floating free from sense: pure insubstantial effect (Womack 1986: 100). Lines 38–45 might also be seen to illustrate this, with their dense but elegant pattern of repetition and contrast of units of sound and sense.

But it is the power of language here, not its vapidity, which summons both fraudsters into existence, and it is language closely associated with money. It is Face's 'credit' (l. 43) which gives Subtle 'countenance' (l. 42), which makes it possible for him to practise his art. The constructed nature of each is soon stressed. Both are, in precise terms, chimerical and protean apparitions created out of the vaporous filth of the city by the alchemical power of money. This is a central idea in the drama. In this opening scene of Act I we see two of the three protagonists of his play summoned into being from worthless fragments and from marginality by the power of money, in the pursuit of money.

But the same can be said of the theatrical experience which the spectators are having at that moment. Behind the façade of both playhouse and Lovewit's house we will be told that there is only:

> The empty walls, worse than I left 'em, smoked,
> A few cracked pots, and glasses, and a furnace;
> The ceiling filled with posies of the candle:
> And Madam, with a dildo, writ o'the walls.
>
> (V, v, 39–42)

Backstage there is also, no doubt, only dust, graffiti and litter. Face and Subtle, in their status as literary creations, in their 'life' in the play and as actors in role, are hollow things of shreds and patches. There is something intensely alive happening here, but it is something insubstantial at the same time. The language both alienates and yet engages its audience's feelings and imagination simultaneously.

As with Face and Subtle, each of the dupes who visit the Blackfriars house is also sharply characterised by the tone and lexis of their conversation: a young lawyer's clerk, Dapper, who wants a 'familiar' to help him cheat at cards but is drawn, blindfolded, into an encounter with Dol as Queen of the Fairies; the taciturn and self-effacing tobacconist Abel Drugger, who, at least initially, seeks magic help in drawing customers into his shop, but is persuaded he can marry above himself and rise to eminence in the city; the vain-glorious and marvellously bombastic Sir Epicure Mammon, whose fantasies of the philosopher's stone are both philanthropic and pornographic, together with his cynical friend Surly; the hilari-ously parodied separatist puritans, the Anabaptists Ananias and Tribulation Wholesome, who seek temporal domination for their sect; and finally Kastril, a country squire come to London to learn to quarrel, accompanied by a very valuable commodity – an attrac-tive, rich, nineteen-year-old widow, Dame Pliant, his sister. All pass in and out of Lovewit's house during a few hectic hours.

The play's most remarkable and important feature is actually its use of time and space. It seems clear that the action takes place in a house in Blackfriars which is located where the theatre stood (Smallwood 1981: 148). A range of specific contemporary refer-ences situate the play in the year of its first performance. Two other references (III, ii, 131–2 and V, v, 102–3) indicate that the action is taking place on either 1 November 1610 or 23 October 1610, depending upon which reference is chosen. Furthermore, *The Alchemist* takes as long to play in the theatre as the time represented by the onstage action, if one accepts that there is a gap of an hour between Acts II and III, as the dialogue indicates (see II, v, 84 and III, ii, 1–2) (Smallwood 1981: 146). The critic Walter Benjamin wrote that 'a clock that is working will always be a disturbance on the stage. Even in a naturalistic play, astronomical time would clash with theatrical time' (Benjamin 1970: 247). Jonson makes the two times not clash, but perfectly coincide.

But if there is a 'disturbance', it is not an estrangement effect where audiences are jolted out of their suspension of disbelief in the theatrical fiction; they never began to believe in the 'reality' of the world in the play. Richard Cave argues that 'Jonson's method is to trap audiences into a sudden . . . perception of the extent to which performance and role play permeate all aspects of human exchange' (Cave 1999a: 58–9). Cave has identified the way in which Jonson's onstage and offstage worlds 'permeate' one another without, I think, that strategy necessarily offering an 'alienation effect' which comments on the offstage world. The two worlds are actually very difficult to separate clearly, if it is possible at all. The coincidence of 'represented' and 'real' time in *The Alchemist* succeeds in almost completely erasing the idea of theatre as a representation of the world, at least in its temporal mode. Jonson's stated aim in the Prologue is 'to better men' (l. 12). His mode of representing time ensures that the audience's moral judgements are exercised in an experience which cannot be dismissed as wholly fictional. This is not a separate imaginary world on another temporal plane into which the audience can look; the time on stage claims to be the same minute of the same day in which the audience are alive. The actor playing Subtle exists in the same moment as that in which the character lives. If this is temporal representation, it is indistinguishable from identity. There is thus a significant sense in which the audience of *The Alchemist* are participants in a kind of game, rather than discrete spectators of a work of art. Players in a game have a different level of moral involvement than mere spectators; whatever moral learning takes place within the game is a first-hand, not vicarious experience for participants.

Jonson's use of time (and, to a lesser extent, place) to efface representation and give the play what the humanists would call its 'ludic' status (see above, p. 12) is a constant, but there are at least three significant moments when the anti-representational strategy is foregrounded: the case of Hieronimo's cloak, Face's implied conspiracy with his master and the play's final lines.

The sceptical gambler Surly has disguised himself as a Spanish count 'to find/ The subtleties of this dark labyrinth' (II, iii, 308) of pretence – typically by a further act of pretence. In this disguise he has met Face at the Temple church and been lured to the house where Dol is ready to seduce him and fleece him of his money (III, iii, 10–23). Face offers the Count to Kastril as a husband for his sister, Dame Pliant, the rich widow whom both Face and Surly now wish to secure for themselves. Even though Surly reveals his true identity to Dame Pliant when they are alone and offers himself as her husband (IV, vi, 1–15), Kastril is convinced that he is an impostor, despite his sister's protestations, and tries out his newly learned quarrelling skills to chase Surly from the house. He is aided by the

Anabaptists, who declare that Surly is wearing 'profane,/ Lewd, superstitious and idolatrous breeches' (IV, vii, 48–9). But a genuine Spanish count has been promised to Kastril, so one will have to be found.

To this end Face now suggests that Drugger might marry Dame Pliant, but he must now dress up as the Spaniard:

> *Face.*   Thou must borrow
> A Spanish suit. Hast thou no credit with the players?
> *Drugger.* Yes, sir, did you never see me play the fool?
> *Face.* I know not, Nab: thou shalt, if I can help it.
> Hieronimo's old cloak, ruff and hat will serve,
> I'll tell thee more, when thou bringst 'em.
>
>   (IV, vii, 67–72)

When Drugger asks Face whether he ever saw him 'play the fool', part of the joke is presumably in the fact that Drugger was being played by Robert Armin, the actor who generally did exactly that for the King's Men (Jonson 1985: 644). This line effaces Armin's representation of Drugger whilst being spoken in role. But the joke is taken further. As suggested in the Induction to *Bartholomew Fair* (l. 94), *The Spanish Tragedy*, probably with Jonson's additions, was still in repertory in 1614 (Kyd 1959: lxvii) and indeed was per- formed at the Fortune as late as 1639 (Gurr 2004: 216). It is not unreasonable to assume that the costume which is fetched by Drugger and later used by Lovewit (V, v) would be recognised by the audience at the Blackfriars in 1610 as the one actually used in performances of Kyd's play at the Globe.

This is not, then, an imitation of Hieronimo's costume as used by the King's Men for performances of *The Spanish Tragedy*; it is the real thing. The world of the play and the 'real' world precisely coincide in this suit of clothes. Its appearance on stage is like that of an animal in a play, which can never of course be 'in role'; it is just itself. As Bert O. States puts it, in such a case: 'the whole enter- prise of theatrical illusionism gets gently debunked,' and we get the perceptual play between the 'real' dog and the dog on stage in a kind of dual perception, 'as with the rabbit/duck sketch of the gestalt psychologists' (States 1983: 380, 381).

Even though the competition for Dame Pliant has irredeemably fractured the venture tripartite, catastrophe strikes before the contest is decided. Lovewit, the master of the house, returns unexpectedly. Face tells Subtle and Doll to take as much of their profits as can be carried and head for Ratcliff in the east where they will meet tomorrow. But at their final meeting Face tells Subtle and Doll (V, iv, 129) that it was he who sent for Lovewit. Robert Smallwood suggests that Face's claim has a 'curious plausibility' (Smallwood 1981: 153). Editors disagree with him (Jonson 1967: 183; 1968: 151; 1987: 220). It is, however, perfectly credible that he is not lying. Act V can be played with Face sure enough of Lovewit's character as an 'indulgent master' (V, iv, 77) to know that he can manipulate him. Lovewit is a man whose eye for the main chance seems similar to his servant's. Face, in summoning Lovewit, can thus ensure that the other two fraudsters have to flee, leaving his master in sole command of what they have gained, and be appropriately rewarded. Certainly Lovewit indicates at the end of the play that he intends to 'help' Face's 'fortune' (V, v, 151). This interpretation would require Face's apparent aside to the audience in Act V scene iii when Lovewit arrives ('What shall I do? I am catch'd' (V, iii, 74)) to be a 'mock' aside to the audience to keep them deceived as long as his colleagues.[4] It would also require Face's asides to the audience, when he admits surprise at hearing Dapper's voice emerge from privy in which he has been hid, blindfolded and gagged with gingerbread (V, iii, 63, 65, 66–7, 68), to be a purely feigned panic. But this series of audacious 'false' asides are immediately prefaced by Face's claim ''tis all *deceptio visus*' (V, iii, 62), a visual deception, a hint to Jonson's favourite kind of audience member, the Latin speaker. But Subtle does warn the audience, in one of the very few moments in the play when he is alone on stage, that 'we must keep Face in awe/ Or he will overlook us like a tyrant' (IV, iii, 18–19). The plural pronoun here encompasses both Subtle and the audience. By the end of the play, as Smallwood notes, Face even seems to be the stage manager, giving the cue for the knock at V, iv, 137. 'Whether the noise precedes or follows the exclamation ["Hark you, thunder!"] is not made clear' (Smallwood 1981: 153). Such an interpretation of Face's relationship to the audience in performance would highlight Face as a deceiver in 'both worlds', on and off stage.

The fact that the offstage backstage and the onstage 'backstage' in *The Alchemist* are simply the same place is shown in a different way when Jonson puts what was behind the stage (the street outside the house) on the stage at the beginning of Act V. Lovewit talks to the neighbours and knocks on the outside of the same door (V, i, 32) which we have previously seen opened from the inside in response to knocks outside (e.g. I, ii, 162).

The concluding lines of *The Alchemist* make the identification of the two worlds even more explicit. As the audience watch Face/Jeremy delivering these lines to them, are they watching the trickster, in role, talking about the next scam which he will set up to deceive new gulls, or the actor pointing out that the money which he has received from the pretence of the performance will enable them to deceive a new audience tomorrow?

> Gentlemen,
> My part fell a little in this last scene,
> Yet 'twas decorum. And though I am clean
> Got off, from Subtle, Surly, Mammon, Dol,
> Hot Ananias, Dapper, Drugger, all
> With whom I traded; yet I put myself
> On you, that are my country: and this pelf,
> Which I have got, if you do quit me, rests
> To feast you often, and invite new guests.
>
> (V, v, 157–65)

Alexander Leggatt remarks that 'there is a disconcerting suggestion that the play is also a con game and we are the victims' (Leggatt 1981: 35). The idea of criminal deception is certainly ratified by Face talking about the audience as if they were a jury (ll. 162–4). But if the effect on the audience of this 'correspondence' is 'scandalous' or 'disconcerting', as Peter Womack suggests (see below, p. 110; Womack 1986: 117), there must be a sense in which the audience are affected by the reality of the 'con' which is being pulled on them; obvious imitations of deceptions do not disconcert. Again we see the process of moral challenge which is typical of Jonson's dramatic strategy in the great middle comedies. How do we feel about our own role in the experience in which we have just taken part? We have enjoyed the con games of the venture tripartite and have delighted in the duping of their customers. How secure, now, is our faith in the moral categories we apply to the business of making money in the modern world, especially if we have been lied to ourselves?

The triumph of Lovewit has made audiences and critics uncomfortable. He readily agrees to overlook the goings-on at the house in his absence in return for the hand of Dame Pliant, having donned Hieronimo's stage costume, and readily claims the remaining swag for himself, threatening and using violence (V, v, 107, 117 s.d.). He even reproaches Surly for not violating Dame Pliant when he had the chance (V, v, 54–5). As Anne Barton writes, he 'seems entirely free from self-delusion or from dissatisfaction with the limits of his existence. This makes him the most formidable, if scarcely the most endearing character in the comedy' (Barton 1984: 150). Julie Sanders suggests that it is because he has consciously avoided being part of the 'Blackfriars community' which has engendered some sympathy through its very communality, even if it inevitably splits (Sanders 1998a: 88). He is not a performer in a play which above all celebrates performance. The most intriguing interpretation of his role has been offered by Andrew Gurr. Gurr argues that the role in the original production must have been taken by the returning joint owner of the Blackfriars theatre, lately come from Stratford to take the profits of the theatrical endeavours of others: William Shakespeare (Gurr 1999: 16–18). Such casting would be entirely consonant with the play's relationship with its material context.

CRITICAL APPROACHES

In the middle decades of the twentieth century a common approach to early modern drama involved a detailed study of the patterns of imagery to be found in the text. Edward B. Partridge's careful image analysis of *The Alchemist* identified 'how thoroughly the implications of the imagery relate business, religion and sex' (Partridge 1958: 149). The comic tone of the play, he considered, comes from the 'monstrous gap' between the extravagance and inflation of the play's metaphorical language and the characters and actions it is being used to describe (Partridge 1958: 157). Partridge's conclu-

sion picked up an idea similar to that found in the earlier work of
L. C. Knights, who argued that the play was an attack on Jacobean
capitalism (Knights 1937). For Partridge,

> the imagery suggests that, in the Alchemist's world, the acqui-
> sition of gold is a religion, a cure-all, a sexual experience, and
> a commercial enterprise . . . Perhaps the true philosopher's
> stone is not the stone itself, but is simply business – that is,
> selling the public the things its wants.
>
> (Partridge 1958: 158)

But 'business', for Partridge, merely exploits a selfish weakness in
'human nature': 'that little world, man, contains the base metals on
which an alchemist can work' (Partridge 1958: 159).

Jonathan Haynes in the 1990s found a more compelling reason to
see the play as a satirical critique, but also paradoxically a celebration of a newly emergent economic system. Previous depictions of
underworld characters on the early modern stage and in the popular
'cony-catching' pamphlets had shown them as a kind of 'anti-
society', aping the roles and professions of 'legitimate' society, and
organised into 'guilds' of thieves and swindlers, each with its own
distinctive argot and hierarchy, in a sort of mirror image of the asso-
ciations of merchants and lawyers. 'Jonson's specific and decisive
step was to imagine an underworld no longer structured on the
guild model, but on a capitalist one' (Haynes 1992: 109). Free-
market London in 1610 required 'a work force in which mobility,
adaptability and imagination were important qualities', the qualities which Dol, Face and Subtle possess in abundance (Haynes
1992: 112). *The Alchemist* has a superficial resemblance to an earlier
genre known as 'estates satire', where the cupidity and folly of representatives of different classes of society are mocked, but where the
distinction between people of different classes is never unsettled.
The Alchemist is written at a time of class insecurity, when rapid
social mobility had made it no longer possible to judge birth
and gentility by appearances alone. Furthermore, knowledge of
how to represent oneself as socially superior had become a commodity in itself, and it is this which the 'venture tripartite' live on
and, fraudulently, by. Their victims' relations with them 'are all

based on unsettled ambitions within the social order and/or on dreams that would explode it, a situation that "greed" only begins to describe' (Haynes 1992: 114). Thus:

> Alchemy is the grand symbol of this volatile state of affairs. The object of limitless desires, it promises infinite wealth and transformative power through operations scarcely less mysterious than the working of capital, whose fantastic logic had not yet been dulled by familiarity. Alchemy makes a neat metaphor for nascent capitalism.
>
> (Haynes 1992: 114)

Face's victory in Act V lies in his ability to take part in a comic settlement which acknowledges the continuing power of the propertied class, as represented by his master Lovewit, 'but does not reject the practices of a new social economy, accommodating it to the strength and durability of the status quo' (Haynes 1992: 117).

It might seem, then, that in conflating criminality and emergent capitalism Jonson is making a political statement. But this is not quite the point: '*The Alchemist* is specific about the terrain of criminal activity without containing and demonizing it within a subculture' (Haynes 1992: 118). The energy which motivates the underworld is the same force which is 'breaking open all social forms' and which gives the play its 'effervescence' (Haynes 1992: 118). Haynes draws no firm moral conclusions about Jonson's intentions: 'it can be read in several ways: he is ironically trying to awaken the audience to the vices it treats as respectable; he is on a badly needed moral holiday; or his moralism has given way to bleak pessimism' (Haynes 1992: 108).

The play's own form represents the economic system which it simultaneously satirises, celebrates and participates in. This has been argued to be a source of *The Alchemist*'s immediacy and energy. Lorna Hutson has pointed out that Lovewit conflates the idea of market, fair and popular theatre in his questions to his neighbours about his butler Jeremy's activities during his absence (V, i, 7–18). Hutson goes on to argue, ingeniously, that the narrative and dramatic structure of City Comedy has much in common with the way a merchant handled a deal; and that, far from condemning the market, it served to legitimise both theatre and market and make them seem 'gentlemanly':

> The ideal of fluency and restraint, of patient withholding and strategic disclosure, which suits the merchant's handling of transactional relations, obviously has much in common with the comic dramatist's technique of holding back part of the story so as to enhance the pleasure of its solution.
>
> (Hutson 1989: 14)

At the same time she acknowledges City Comedy's sense that the market and City Comedy are both offering unlimited opportunities and 'the inescapable conviction of having been deceived' (Hutson 1989: 12). Similarly, Susan Wells sees accumulation as the economic mode of *The Alchemist*: 'The play develops *through* unbridled accumulation, as various characters try to outwit and swindle each other; it is a transparent assumption of the play.' Yet the actions of the venture tripartite, 'as Knights pointed out long ago, are funniest and most understandable when seen through the lens of an anti-accumulationist ethic' (Wells 1981: 54, 56). The play condemns, and yet is wonderfully animated by, the dynamic of the market.

Peter Womack finds the play to be not so ambivalent in its attitude. As other critics have noticed, Lovewit's house 'as its name neatly hints, is a self-referring image of the theatre' (Womack 1986: 118). But for Womack, Jonson makes the theatre a house of cheaters, and the image is 'disgraceful and cynical' (Womack 1986: 118). Here he picks up the idea of Jonson's distaste for the theatre which is also found in the work of the American critic Jonas A. Barish.[5] Womack conflates Jonson's classicism with a specific mode of understanding the world emergent at this time which the French philosopher Michel Foucault also called 'Classicism'. The scientific, empiricist and positivist assumptions to be found in the work of, for example, Jonson's friend Francis Bacon typify this nascent 'enlightenment' way of thinking. This 'Classical Episteme', as Foucault called it, has a 'monolinear conception of reality, leaving [theatrical] performance with nothing to do but represent that reality, and nothing to *be* but unreal'. Acting itself becomes not only inauthentic, but 'furtive and silly' (Womack 1986: 109). The scandal of the theatre, as expressed in *The Alchemist*, writes Womack, is that it is 'definingly *illicit*'; it does not copy nature or instruct, but rather exploits 'the fantasies of its clients to get away with flagrant violations of probability'.[6] Actors are 'the peers, not of the grave orator, but of jugglers and whores. Acting is detached from the official art of rhetoric, and assimilated, in particular, to two unofficial, transgressive codes: that of sex, and that of alchemy' (Womack 1986: 118).

To take the latter first, because alchemy as a 'science' depends upon the interpretation of a system of arcane correspondences between things only visible to the adept, as opposed to the straightforward empiricism of enlightenment thinking, it is 'a theatrical language in the sense that within it, words and things are not blankly what they are . . . it's a polysemous code, intentionally generating covert meanings' (Womack 1986: 128). A satire on alchemy becomes a satire on theatre itself.

With regard to sexual transgression, Womack argues that the play's ending is a scandalous parody of a conventional comic ending. Dame Pliant marries the Spanish Count, who happens at the moment to be Lovewit, but three other characters (Surly, Drugger and Face) have worn or intended to wear the costume. 'Hardly anyone believes that he exists in the normal sense, but the criss-crossing inventions concerning him invest him in a delusive actuality.' Thus the conclusion 'effects an opportunistic accommodation between authority and illusion. So far from being a Shakespearean vindication of an authentic relationship, the wedding is a con-man's masterstroke' (Womack 1986: 119). Womack then goes on to argue that the masculine self, which is supposed to be integrated, rational, self-contained and physically assertive ('constructed by grammar and violence'), becomes dispersed in the play's 'multiple roles, polysemy, transmutation' (Womack 1986: 125). He discusses here Face's 'extraordinary celebration of the sexual reprocessing of the Spanish grandee' (III, iii, 41–9) (Womack 1986: 125), but he could also consider Mammon's sexual fantasy of his image being dispersed and lost in a perfumed mist (II, ii, 45–50). Such a 'psychic release' produces a 'disreputable euphoria' of tone in both these speeches (Womack 1986: 125). 'Sexual energy becomes a generator of illusion, a specifically theatrical productivity' (Womack 1986: 126). The opposite may well also be true; Jonsonian illusion can seem very erotically charged for the spectator at times, too.

Womack argues that the theatricalisation of the male produces his sexuality as a 'form of paranoia' (Womack 1986: 125); but the play's females can still be seen as primarily male possessions. Julie Sanders finds *The Alchemist* to be perhaps Jonson's 'most egalitarian (republican?) dramatic gesture' (Sanders 1998a: 72) in that Face and Subtle have to collaborate for success. There is between them a struggle as each competes for 'the position of absolute monarch in this city-state, Subtle adopting the title of "Sovereign", Face more cynically adopting the "republican" cover of "general"' (Sanders 1998a: 76). Dol is clever enough to identify both the inbuilt weaknesses of this political system, warning Mammon of the danger of the combination of both democratic and absolutist forces in a state (IV, iv, 147–50). She also predicts civil war in the future (I, i, 82), 'an extraordinarily prescient statement for 1610' (Sanders 1998a: 74). Yet, writes Sanders, as a woman she remains 'the plebeian element of this oligarchical republic' (Sanders 1998a: 74). 'Her body can be purchased by anyone with the necessary capital. She is indeed the republican epitome of a "public thing", *the res publica*', as she calls herself at I, i, 110 (Sanders 1998a: 73). Her playing of roles is not seen as any threat to the social hierarchy, as Face observes when he calls it 'a kind of modern happiness, to have/ Dol Common for a great lady' (IV, i, 23–4). Mares (Jonson 1967: 124) glosses these lines as 'it is fitting for these degenerate dates that a prostitute should be taken for a great lady,' but Anne Barton reads the words 'modern happiness' to have their contemporary meanings and writes that 'the play as a whole suggests, and even seems to endorse, the truth underlying Face's . . . observation' (Barton 1984: 153):

> Jonson has employed the most sordid, the most meticulous realistic material, and defiantly extracted from it a kind of gold of the imagination. Language has . . . contracted the whole world, as it seems, and made it live fully for a few hours within the walls of a stripped and deserted house – or a theatre. There is nothing restrained, ordered or balanced about life in *The*

Alchemist, and no suggestions are put forward as to how any reforms in that direction might be effected.

(Barton 1984: 152)

The play reveals and revels in the theatricality of the world and the worldliness of theatre.

THE PLAY IN PERFORMANCE

Sam Mendes directed his first Jonson, *The Alchemist*, for the RSC in 1991. After a difficult first read-through, where the actors made very little sense at all of the script, a breakthrough was made:

> Suddenly something happens, something clicks: they begin to understand the rhythm of it and it becomes terribly translu-cent, and very easily understandable. Structurally I think *The Alchemist* is very, very fine. The key to it lies partly in under-standing that there's a rhythm not just in specific scenes but throughout the whole play; there's a rhythmical mainstream to *The Alchemist* as there is to all of his plays. If you tap it, if you can get on the back of it, it's remarkably powerful
>
> (Mendes 1999: 79–80).

Once Mendes's production was running he found that it lasted pre-cisely two hours twenty-three minutes over forty performances (Mendes 1999: 82). Ian Donaldson has written of this play as Jonson's 'clockwork comedy'; 'its design is cleverer, more intricate, more elegant, more surprising than that of any comedy by Shakespeare; it is as cunning as clockwork' (Donaldson 1997: 89). The plot of *The Alchemist* may well possess the features of an intricate timepiece, but successful performance of the play also seems to depend upon tapping into the 'rhythmical mainstream' of Jonson's writing.

The earliest hint of the need for absolute precision in pace, timing and expense of energy comes in an anonymous prologue written for the play's Restoration revival in 1660. Having doubted whether modern actors could do justice to the part of Dol, the writer describes the roles of Face and Subtle as

> parts, all air, and fire:
> They, whom the author did himself inspire,
> Taught, line by line, each tittle, accent, word . . .
>   (Noyes 1935: 105; HSS IX: 227–8)

There is an intriguing suggestion here that Jonson himself may have supervised the precise delivery of the lines in the original performance, with an emphasis on the precise sound made by the actor for each word.

There is a pulse of raw physical energy in this play's language which interacts beautifully with the intricate musicality of the language. Jean Gascon, in a programme note to his acclaimed 1969 production for the Stratford Festival Production of Canada, described Jonson as 'Rabelais and Johann Sebastian Bach rolled into one' (Jensen 1985: 103).[7] The visceral, Rabelaisian experience of the play in full flow is well described by Martin Armstrong reviewing the 1923 London production by the Phoenix Society: 'Jonson's laughter is bracing, natural thunder . . . though intellect guides it is directed at the midriff first, only afterwards at the head, but it never lacks the majesty of course or a flowing fecundity of invention' (Jensen 1985: 85).

The history of *The Alchemist* in performance demonstrates that those who have put their trust in the experience of hearing the play's language, obscurities and all, and let its hocus-pocus words work on the hungry, hopeful gullibility of both Subtle's customers and of the audience, have triumphed. Mendes's production was 'exhilarating', wrote Michael Billington, because it put 'the emphasis where it should be: on the feverish richness of Jonson's language and the farcical brilliance of his plot' (*The Guardian*, 17 April 1992: 32). Cluttered sets, extraneous 'business' and 'updated' language are the marks of less successful productions. The central feature of the set of Bill Alexander's 1996 National Theatre production was some kind of huge alchemical apparatus, but it gave the impression that 'some mad blacksmith [had] made scores of cogs, spanners, pipes, radiators and candlesticks and a few instruments of torture' (*The Times*, 18 September 1996: 34).[8] The actors were constrained by this structure and acted around it, in what was, according to Sheridan Morley in *The Spectator*, consequently 'a curiously lifeless evening'

(*The Spectator*, 19 October 1996). The play, however, constitutes its own machine and needs no physical representation of its own processes. As Richard Cave writes of this production, 'it is the spiralling of over-heated minds that should astonish, delight and shock audiences, not arabesques of wrought ironwork' (Cave 1999: 56). The production was 'brash and, most of the time, . . . farcical' (*The Times*, 18 September 1996: 34). This was a cardinal error. Farce is indeed primarily about plot and timing, but poetry and meta-theatricality are equally crucial to *The Alchemist*. Tyrone Guthrie in 1962 also mistakenly saw the play as 'really a farce' and freely updated the language, costumes and setting. Some, including Kenneth Tynan, thought the production a triumph (Jensen 1985: 94–5). But many were far more critical. Bamber Gascoigne in *The Spectator*, in a savage review, pointed out that successfully updating *The Alchemist* would actually 'require a twentieth-century Ben Jonson' (*The Spectator*, 7 December 1962).[9] Bernard Levin in his review declared that Jonson's play 'is far *more* timely, modern, up to date in its own dress and language than in this wearisome, bastard tongue' (Jensen 1985: 95). The texture of the play's language is crucial to its theatrical effect. The director Nicholas Hytner at the National Theatre in 2006 would not trust that language, as an account of the rehearsal process explains:

> 'If we can't make clear what something means,' said Hytner, 'cut it.' Nothing was allowed to be obscure. He had given the company the single reason why people were going to come and see this play. 'Because it's funny,' he said. 'It has to be funny.'
>
> (Butler 2006: 38)

Given that so much of the play's diction and action can seem obscure, the director's attitude may be the reason why the actors seemed to lose faith in the play's texture of sound. By late in the run they were getting almost all their laughs from stage business and ad libs rather than letting the text work. Ian Richardson's Mammon was a rare exception. Consequently the production caused the audience to chuckle politely, instead of producing, as it can, 'just one laugh after another after another. And that's in the writing' (Mendes 1999: 82).

Very many reviews of modern productions point out that the play's subject matter has a contemporary relevance for its audience (Jensen 1985: 79, 83, 86, 87, 89, 106, 107). It was apparently the notorious South Sea Bubble Scandal of the 1720s which restored this comedy to popularity in the eighteenth century after a period of neglect (Noyes 1935: 115). There is certainly an immediacy about *The Alchemist* in performance, but it is superficial to ascribe that powerful sense of 'relevance' to the fact that financial swindles are ever-present scandals in capitalist societies. The contemporary feel of the play in performance is more a product of a meta-theatricality which rests on two conceits. The first relates alchemy with acting; the second suggests that the commercial theatre on one level is a scam to deprive its credulous audience of their money, in form the same as the capitalist economy of which it is an immediate, living part, or a game in which only one side, the actors, can win. In Trevor Nunn's 1977 RSC production this latter point was well brought out by Ian McKellen's Face when speaking the play's final lines (V, v, 163–5; see above, pp. 105–6 and Fig. 6.1). As he spoke the lines McKellen, according to the theatre critic Rosemary Say, 'clinks his ill-gotten coins slowly through his fingers and sizes up the audience in front of him' (Leggatt 1981: 283). Richard Cave noted that this particular *Alchemist* triumphed because 'there was a heart-stopping precariousness about it all . . . it was exhilarating because it was all *felt* to be dangerous' (Cave 1991: 92). In all deceptions, because there is the ever-present danger of discovery, there is a sense of living life in the moment. The greater the consequences of immediate failure or exposure as a fraud or fool, the more intense the experience. In the plague-ridden moment of the original production (see above, p. 97), and in the full knowledge that the crimes of the 'venture tripartite' were capital ones, the first *Alchemist* had a precarious context for both audience and characters which no 'modernisation' can reproduce. Deception also needs to move fast to avoid examination. For Face, Subtle and Dol, 'the quickly doing of it is the grace' (IV, iii, 104). As Ian Donaldson writes, 'speed is the secret of their survival, as it is of their deceptions' (Donaldson 1997: 96). Just as the tricksters must be speedy, the play requires pace and energy to carry its audience through its linguistic smokescreen of

6.1 Susan Fleetwood as Dol Common and Ian McKellen as Face in *The Alchemist*, The Other Place, Stratford-upon-Avon, 1977. Reg Wilson © Royal Shakespeare Company.

jargon-filled nonsense (Donaldson 1978: 213–14); the two go together. The 2006 National Theatre production really lost its way when Doll, Face and Subtle settled down for a tea break in Act III scene iii.

Such an intense feeling of precariousness should be common to the onstage characters and their audience when the play's meta-theatre is fully realised and the audience fully involved. Some modern anti-theatricalists are embarrassed by the stage because, unlike the screen, the performance might fail publicly at any time. In the early modern theatre the audience are not hidden in the dark from each other but exposed as part of the spectacle of other spectators. A crucial weakness of the 2006 National Theatre production was the 8-metre gap between the front of the revolving set and the front row of the Olivier stalls. The blurring of the boundaries between the offstage and onstage includes the audience in the dangerous moment, makes them even more aware of the twin levels of precariousness which operate. The three tricksters are forever on the verge of being found out; the audience are even more than usually aware that this is a play which may fail in front of them. They may also feel at the end that Face or the Olympian figure of the playwright may be laughing at them as he takes their money.

The Alchemist is a play about how utopian yearning can render us all foolish, as the vast energy of the characters and their language clashes against the formal time scheme of the play, a structure which depicts 'a world amenable to explanation, in which events move more or less rationally through various stages of crisis and denouncement to a given end' (Donaldson 1997: 105).

If the play is a finely tuned machine it takes a sensitive director and an ensemble cast to set it working. If the process is successful the audience will be absorbed into its workings and will experience at first hand a central insight of the drama. Just like the play, the economic system we live trapped in is an exploitative historical process running in real time; but the play's formal eloquence, excitement and energy, above all manifested in delightful laughter, express the hopes, for now apparently deluded, of human beings for a future world outside this ticking machine.

NOTES

1. The case for the Blackfriars is well made in Smallwood 1981: 147–8. See also Jonson 1967: lx and Donaldson 1997: 82–3. HSS (IX: 223) assert that the Globe was the site of the first performance.
2. See Wells 1981: 42; Agnew 1986: 50; Gurr 1992: 118; Mullaney 1991.
3. For a brief account of theory and processes of alchemy see Jonson 1967: xxxi–xl.
4. If the line is an aside at all. Jonson sometimes used brackets to indicate an aside either to the audience or to another character. The line is not in brackets in the 1609 Quarto, unlike others in the scene.
5. See, for example, Barish 1973a.
6. It should be noted that Jonson claims that he is doing the opposite of this in 'To the Reader' (ll. 1–8) and 'Prologue' (ll. 11–24).
7. See also Peter Barnes's comments on p. 69 above. There are obvious similarities with the way *Volpone* has been successfully played (see above, pp. 68–9).
8. The production originated at the Birmingham Repertory Theatre. See also the review of the comparable 1966 New York production in Jensen 1985: 99–100.
9. Reprinted in Holdsworth 1978: 226–9.

CHAPTER 7

Bartholomew Fair (1614)

*B*artholomew Fair is a complex meditation on the place of the theatre in the politics of Jacobean London.

CONTEXTS

The play was first performed at the newly built Hope playhouse on Bankside on 31 October 1614, and subsequently the following evening at court before the King. Jonson sought to address both city and court simultaneously; the comedy is formed by the political tension which existed between those two centres of power that autumn.

The stage at the Hope was a temporary construction on trestles, lacking the canopy which was a feature of public playhouses such as the Globe. The pit was also used for bear-baiting on alternate days. After 1616 the Hope was entirely given over to that sport (Marcus 1986: 43). Bartholomew Fair, which is represented on stage in four of the play's five acts, was itself the site of theatrical performance (including puppet shows) on trestle stages in similarly insalubrious surroundings. Jonson has the Scrivener point out, in the Induction written for the performance at the Hope, that 'the Author hath observed a special decorum, the place being as dirty as Smithfield and as stinking every whit' (Ind., ll. 139–40). This 'special decorum' of Bankside playhouse/bear-pit as Smithfield fairground is an important aspect of the comedy's playfulness about its location, both dramaturgical and political.

If the smell and environment of the Hope directly recalled Bartholomew Fair, it seems as if Jonson, unusually, went even further in seeking a representational 'set' for this production. At the court performance the following night we know that payment was made for 'canvas for the booths and other necessaries for a play called *Bartholomew Fair*' (HSS IX: 245). Hints in the Induction (ll. 18–19, 21) make it seem more than likely that booths representing Ursla the pig woman's tent and Lantern Leatherhead's 'shop', as well as Joan Trash's gingerbread stall, appeared on stage at least during Acts II, III and IV (Jonson 1963: 206). No other of Jonson's plays had so far required a specific 'set' of this kind. Eugene M. Waith has suggested that the appearance of these three 'houses' at the back of the platform recalled both the emblematic 'simultaneous staging' of medieval drama, where several locations ('mansions') were all represented on stage at the same time, and the street of houses commonly used as a setting by the Roman comic dramatists Plautus and Terence (Jonson 1963: 217). Another analogy may also have been evident at the Hope. 'Realistic', representational staging was a feature of the court masque. The Induction cheekily proposes that the audience are not courtiers, but paying customers who are participants in a commercial contract (ll. 52ff). The staging conventions of court performance are, on the occasion of the first performance, assertively brought into the suburbs; the ways of seeing the world of the court and of the city are to be in awkward juxtaposition, as they are throughout the play.

Smithfield, lying just outside the north-eastern city walls, had been the site of a three-day cloth fair in the grounds of St Bartholomew the Great every August since the twelfth century. By 1614 the Fair was more noted as a site of late summer entertainment and revelry for the masses (see I, v, 117–18) than for its economic importance. The fair's charter, originally granted by Henry II, offered it 'a curious legal position' which left it to some extent outside royal control; 'like a commonly used road on private property, the public gained some rights on it and it could not be closed by fiat.' The fair, writes Frances Teague, 'which cut across society, was beyond the normal rules of society' (Teague 1985: 20, 21).

Justice Overdo sits as a magistrate for one of the fair's own courts ('Pie-powders', II, i, 37) outside the normal legal system, a tribunal which in reality employed a jury of tradesmen from the fair to ensure equitable dealing.

The theatre, and other holiday pastimes and sports, enjoyed the support and patronage of the court but not of the city authorities. *Bartholomew Fair*, a drama written for the King's entertainment on All Saints' Night, makes a play of the city's own festival. Leah Marcus has argued that the London Corporation, which otherwise was hostile both ideologically and administratively to the theatre, took the profits from the 'pleasure fair' at Smithfield and hypocritically gained from puppet shows, ballad-singers, bawdry and general festivity: debased forms of theatre. Jonson's purpose, she suggests, is that 'sober sorts who shrink from the vanities of the playhouse while allowing themselves to profit from the vanities of the fair' should 'look on their motives' (Marcus 1986: 42). She has also suggested that the play takes sides with King James in his struggles with the city and its allies in Parliament and the judiciary in more specific ways.

Puritan opposition to James meant that the King could not rely upon Parliament for his income. In early 1614 James had summoned the legislature and offered it his 'love' in the hope of subsidy being granted. None was forthcoming, but a bill forbidding bear-baiting and morris dancing on the sabbath was passed (Marcus 1986: 49). Parliament was dissolved after two months. James attempted to use the royal prerogative in collecting taxes – for example, on new buildings – but was opposed by the judiciary, including Chief Justice Coke, who upheld the common law in the face of what were seen as unconstitutional acts on the part of the monarch. Adam Overdo, Marcus demonstrates, is a satirical portrait of a justice 'who consistently places the law before the king and assumes that he is its only true interpreter' (Marcus 1986: 54). His motto makes clear his sense of priorities: 'in justice's name, and the King's; and for the commonwealth' (II, i, 41–2). Ultimately his conduct shows him to be more concerned with his own status and self-gratification than with justice, and he abuses his wardship of Grace by planning to marry her off to his brother-in-law, the idiotic Bartholomew Cokes, thus keeping her money in his control (III, v,

254–6; Marcus 1986: 55).[1] For most of the play Overdo is in disguise so that he can secretly observe the 'enormities' of the fairground people. Here Jonson is making use of the convention of the disguised ruler found in Shakespeare's *Measure for Measure* (1604) and Marston's *The Malcontent* (printed 1604). Jonson makes the disguised ruler himself the object of the audience's observation not solely for a dramaturgical technique, dramatic irony, but so that the real, unseen King's authority may be strengthened in the world of which the play is a part, Marcus argues.

The funniest satirical target of *Bartholomew Fair* is another of the King's opponents, the self-righteous Sabbatarian Puritan, seen here in the shape of Zeal-of-the-land Busy. The historian Patrick Collinson has suggested that Jonson's powerful creation of the stage Puritan, both in this play and *The Alchemist*, was widely influential, even in the way in which Puritans saw themselves (Collinson 1995: 164–9).[2] As Peter Lake puts it, these 'negative images did intersect with and help to shape the self-projection and protection mechanisms with which the godly subsequently sought to meet the challenge of what they took to be a hostile world' (Lake 2002: 582). Both historians acknowledge the contemporary force of Jonson's brilliant satire. As in the case of Adam Overdo, hypocrisy is the prime quality. Busy's language precisely echoes biblical grammar and collocations, with the cadences and rhythms of contemporary sermonising (Barish 1960: 199). In a memorable piece of casuistry Busy justifies the eating of pork at the fair in the manner in which Puritans demonstrated the righteousness of their every action with characteristic logic chopping (I, vi, 43–85; see Barish 1960: 201–2; Lake 2002: 585–7). Busy is an enemy of idolatry[3] but 'surrounds himself with pseudo-sacramental foodstuffs' (Marcus 1986: 51). An inflated, grotesque version of the 'godly' preacher, Busy finds the anti-Christ of Catholicism in any kind of traditional pastime. He finds demonic features in innocent objects such as gingerbread men, railing against superstition out of superstitious fear of the past.

At the old medieval fair disputations took place between theological students. In the play's climax, Busy is defeated and silenced by a puppet. A standard Puritan argument against the theatre was that some actors dressed as women, an 'abomination' specifically condemned in the Bible (Deut. 22: 5). The puppet Dionysus in Leatherhead's puppet show of *Hero and Leander* raises his garment to show that he is 'neither male nor female' and so the biblical injunction does not apply. Busy is humiliated and changed by his experience of the fair, as are all the other visitors to some degree.

The Prologue which Jonson wrote for the court performance promised the King satire of 'your land's faction . . . whereof the petulant ways/ Yourself have known, and have been vexed with long' (ll. 4, 6–7). Marcus later refined her reading of Jonson's depiction of Busy, seeing in him a reflection of what she takes to be Jonson's own latent anti-theatricality. She has come to see in the play's energy a subconscious delight in law-breaking which bursts out of the contractual requirement for law-keeping which has apparently been spelled out so clearly in the Induction (Marcus 1995: 174–81). Whatever Jonson's intentions for the play, overt or subconscious, its subject matter is the contest for authority in the state; its form is concerned with moral authority in the playhouse.[4]

THE PLAY

T. S. Eliot claimed that *Bartholomew Fair* 'hardly' had a plot at all; 'the marvel of the play', he wrote, is the 'bewildering rapid action' (Eliot 1951: 155). In fact the careful structuring of the action is as intricate as the plotting of *Volpone* or *The Alchemist*.

As Richard Levin explained, at the heart of the play are the actions of two different but parallel groups of middle-class visitors to the fair (Levin 1971: 203). Act I takes place at the house of the leader of one group, John Littlewit the proctor (an agent in the church courts). His pregnant wife Win-the-fight has an urge to eat roasted pig at the fair, and her husband prevails upon the ludicrous and gluttonous Zeal-of-the-land Busy to approve the visit, under certain conditions. Busy is staying at Littlewit's house as a suitor to Win's widowed mother, Dame Purecraft. Two members of the second group visit Littlewit's house during the opening act: the idiotic squire of Harrow, Bartholomew Cokes, and his ill-tempered tutor, Humphrey Wasp. They have come to collect a licence for Cokes to marry the ward Grace Wellborn. Grace and her guardian's wife, Dame Alice Overdo, complete the second quartet. There is a clear parallelism between the two groups: Littlewit and Cokes as apparent leaders, though both fools, and in fact under the nominal authority of Busy and Wasp, who are both outspoken haters of the Fair. There are also two women with suitors, and two married and apparently respectable women, both of whom tend to do as they are bid. The Littlewit party is urban and disingenuous, the Cokes party rural and relatively naive (Levin 1971: 205).

Levin further demonstrates that as the two parties visit the fair and its delights the groups disintegrate, only to reform into pairs of equivalent characters in the final act for the play's resolution (Levin 1971: 208). Their encounter with the hucksters, ballad-sellers, prostitutes and pickpockets effects a kind of transformation on all of them. Littlewit and Cokes are freed from their censorious guardians; Wasp and Busy both relinquish their authority and endure a spell in the stocks. The shame alone is enough for Wasp to declare that 'the date of my authority is out' (V, iv, 85–6). Busy attacks the puppet show of *Hero and Leander* which Cokes puts on for all the play's characters in the final act as an 'abomination', only to be defeated (see above, p. 123). Grace and Dame Purecraft find themselves with husbands (Winwife and Quarlous) more desirable than the suitors with which they began the play, and Win and Dame Overdo have become drunk and fallen in with pimps – though they do return to their husbands.

There is thus an order and pattern similar to *Volpone* or *The Alchemist* where tricksters are visited by a variety of characters only for the visitors all to be brought together in the final scene where home truths are revealed to almost all of them. Instead of a Face or Volpone orchestrating matters, however, for Levin there is only the 'author's hand shaping the material to create an equivalent sense of pace and pattern' (Levin 1971: 208). Quarlous does, however, step in to direct the action in the final scenes.

In the final act the cast of the play themselves become an audience of the puppet play, provoking the theatre audience to consider what it is to sit in judgement of a performance. Richard Cave sums up the fifth act as follows:

> Like confronts like. Jonson has contrived to make the art of performance a metaphysical conceit for the essential nature of

every human activity on the grounds that all relations involve observation, insight, generosity – the attributes that determine the quality of the response we term judgement. Jonson simultaneously presents us with an image of the world we inhabit and dramatises the complexity of our relation to it to forestall too prompt and easy a response.

(Cave 1991: 117)

These concerns are clearly signalled in the play's remarkable Induction. In that scene we are reminded that theatre is not merely a product for consumption; if we reduce our right and capacity to make judgements about what we see to a market relationship we abandon the theatre's essentially moral nature. When, in the Induction, the Scrivener proposes that the value of the judgement of each member of the audience should depend upon how much they each paid to get in (Ind., ll. 75–85), Jonson is surely being satirical. The Scrivener reads out a contract to the audience ('articles drawn out in haste between our author and you'; Ind., ll. 53–4). But in the play proper which follows, market-based contractualism is presented as irrational and amoral, if not a means of bullying. In the play's very first speech Littlewit points out that the jokes of a man who has only drunk cheap beer can surpass the wit of those who 'pay twopence in a quart more for their canary than other men' (I, i, 32–3); you don't necessarily get what you pay for. But there are also three amoral contracts drawn up in the play. The Scrivener's articles are 'indented' (Ind., l. 57) and 'covenanted' (ll. 64, 100); the agreement that the ballad-singer Nightingale will assemble a crowd for the cutpurse Edgworth to prey on and then direct him to the most suitable target (II, iv, 31–9) is also described by Ursla the pig woman as an 'indenture' and a 'covenant' (II, iv, 41–2). Quarlous observes this confederacy at work, and then uses this knowledge to blackmail Edgworth into stealing for him the box containing Grace's marriage licence from Wasp. Quarlous knows that he places himself in danger of being an accessory to robbery, but makes a deal to their mutual benefit (III, v, 223–38). Edgworth certainly sees it as a contract where his good name is at stake if he defaults (ll. 243–4), and does fulfil his side of the bargain. Ultimately, Quarlous's capture of Grace's wardship, which ensures him the payment of her estate on her marriage to Winwife (V, vi, 78), is down to a legal contract in the form of Adam Overdo's grant of a blank warrant on which he may write 'anything . . . that thou wantst now or any time hereafter' above the justice's signature: 'it is my deed, I deliver it so' (V, ii, 105). Quarlous is disguised as the madman Troubleall, but thanks to another effective blackmail on Quarlous's part (V, vi, 89–92), it is not in Overdo's interest to challenge the written contract when it is made public. Contractualism is the subject of the satire.

The contrasting roles and functions of Justice Adam Overdo and Tom Quarlous are central to the drama's effect and to the question of the audience's engagement with the action. The meta-theatrical aspects of the text deserve close examination. The Induction begins with a typical challenge to the audience to distinguish between the world-in-the-play and the play-in-the-world. The stage-keeper enters and pleads with the audience:

> Gentlemen, have a little patience, they are e'en upon coming, instantly. He that should begin the play, Master Littlewit the proctor, hath a stitch new fall'n in his black silk stocking; 'twill be drawn up ere you can tell twenty.
>
> (Ind., ll. 1–4)

It is not immediately obvious whether this is an actual stage-keeper apologising for the late start of the play, or an actor playing the role of the stage-keeper speaking a script; in fact, it does not matter. The Induction does not act as an alienating framing device such as may be operating in Shakespeare's *The Taming of the Shrew* or Marston's *The Malcontent*. There is normally no pretence in Jonson's middle comedies that the characters are engaged in a self-contained world separated from the audience (see above, p. 14). The opening lines of the Induction establish this convention. What is surprising, however, is that Adam Overdo, the deluded moral commentator on the action, does seem to exist in just such a separate world.

Act III scene iii consists almost entirely of Adam Overdo reflecting at length upon the beating which he received at the hands of Wasp (II, vi, 125–37), having been suspected of the first pick-pocketing of Cokes by the cutpurse Edgworth (II, vi, 52). On stage, unseen with him and overhearing, are Quarlous and Winwife.[5] At the conclusion of the speech Winwife turns to his friend and asks 'What [i.e. why] does he talk to himself and act so seriously? Poor fool!' (III, iii, 35–6). Overdo, it seems, talks to himself and not to the audience.

Quarlous and Winwife are two gallants who stand outside of the play's principal structure. Winwife is a visitor to Littlewit's house as a suitor to Dame Purecraft in Act I and Quarlous is his friend, but they are not interested in the fair itself. They originally go to observe the antics of Cokes and his crowd for their own amusement (I, v, 124–6). Quarlous's motivation in the play may then be said to be the same as ours. Levin regards them as 'our representatives at the fair, guiding our response, in the manner of a chorus, to the comic behaviour it brings out in the Cokes and Littlewit parties' (Levin 1971: 207). They stand then in the role that Adam Overdo would be expected to have if he were not so myopic and easily fooled.

A reason for his failure to exert this choric role is strongly suggested by Winwife's comment at the end of Act III scene iii. Either Winwife is so isolated within the world-in-the-play that he is not aware of the audience, or the same is true of Adam Overdo. But Winwife himself does address the audience, it would seem, soon after, when he suspects his friend of angling after Grace ('Ay, Master Quarlous, are you proffering?' . . . 'I'll look to you i'faith, gamester'; III, v, 260, 262). Either that or he is talking to himself, the very thing he finds strange in Overdo in Act III scene iii. It must be that Justice Overdo has been talking to himself and not the audience, whenever he is not addressing other characters onstage. This is indeed the case in his opening speech in the play, when he is alone onstage at the beginning of Act II: 'Well, in justice's name, and the King's, and for the commonwealth! Defy all the world, Adam Overdo, for a disguise, and all story; for thou hast fitted thyself, I swear' (II, i, 1–3). If this is right, then the figure of 'justice' in the play is wholly lost in the represented world-in-the-play, mumbling to himself in a delusion that has no connection with the world of the other characters or of the audience, and in defiance of the conventions of the lone speaker on the early modern stage.[6] Hence Winwife's bemused comment which surely must draw a laugh from the audience: 'What does he talk to himself?'

Genuine audience address is first granted to Grace, where she expresses her desire to avoid marriage with Cokes (I, v, 76–7).

Largely, however, Jonson scripts audience contact for the most rascally characters. Edgworth not only boasts to the audience of his intent of robbing Cokes (II, vi, 117), but also enjoys a genuine, funny twenty-three line soliloquy with some good jokes at the expense of the foolish Harrow squire (IV, ii, 46–58). Even Cokes is given a chance to address the audience in soliloquy immediately afterwards, perhaps generating some sympathy; very likely the audience are the recipients of his discarded pears (IV, ii, 65). In the final scenes of the play, however, it is Quarlous who works hardest to acquire the audience's approval as he seizes control of a plot which has hitherto lacked an onstage guiding intelligence.

Quarlous stands out from the rest in the complexity of his characterisation and in his energetic unpleasantness.[7] In his opening scene, having got Littlewit drunk the night before, he now takes the opportunity to fondle and proposition his wife (I, iii, 25–50) before embarking upon a graphic and misogynistic comic rant about the perils of sex with older women (I, iii, 55–72). And yet his views on Puritans sound very Jonsonian, since Busy 'derides all antiquity' and 'defies any other learning than inspiration' (I, iii, 126). For most of the play Quarlous is determined to set himself apart from the other characters and act as an amused spectator. He lives up to his name when invited to become more involved with the actions of the play itself. Quarlous reminds us of his Oxford education when, employing sarcastic classical allusions, he laughs at the fair (II, v, 6–15) and rudely disdains the horse dealer Knockem, with whom he is obviously acquainted (II, v, 29–34). He ridicules Ursla the pig woman's appearance with characteristic hyperbole (II, v, 72–88), and insists on pursuing the quarrel until he ends by striking Knockem. Ursla's leg is scalded in the mêlée which follows. Yet he makes the audience laugh, and succeeds in disrupting the activities of the fair and injuring its people. When, in the scene immediately following, Adam Overdo offers his own, more principled if pompous criticism of the fair's delights – and specifically 'bottle-ale and tobacco' (II, vi, 1) – the Justice's speech becomes an occasion for Edgworth to pick the distracted Cokes's pocket. When the theft is discovered Cokes's tutor Wasp beats him offstage, accusing him of complicity in the theft (II, vi, 127). Both Quarlous and Overdo disdain the fair, but only Quarlous is able to have some impact upon it, and upon the audience.

The gallant's position as an effective critic both inside and outside of the onstage action at this point is spelled out at his next entrance when Quarlous tells Winwife that, though he wishes he had seen Cokes's robbery, 'the best is that we shall have five acts of him ere night; he'll be spectacle enough' (III, ii, 2–3). They do get to see Edgworth make a victim of Cokes again and watch as engaged spectators; indeed Quarlous enjoys the show, calling out excitedly when the thief struggles to find his prey: 'Good, i'faith! Oh, he has lighted on the wrong pocket' (III, v, 148).

Among the other onstage spectators is Grace Wellborn, and Quarlous soon becomes involved in a competition with his friend for the rich ward's favours. There is thus a new plot development which is outside of any involvement with the fair itself. Its inception coincides with the discrediting in the eyes of the audience of the moral credentials of Justice Overdo; he bought Grace's wardship for the purpose of marrying her off to his wife's stupid brother, an arrangement which will leave him in control of the wealth attached to her, and a union which she cannot avoid without paying the value of that wealth to her guardian (III, v, 254–6). But Quarlous has already compromised his independence from the fair and he will not now be able to continue to play meta-theatrical games with the audience. He has employed Edgworth to steal the box containing the licence to marry Grace which Wasp had collected from Littlewit in Act I (III, vi, 220–45). He justifies the act in terms of spectatorial pleasure at the time ('I would fain see the careful fool deluded', l. 246), but once he is involved with the fair people his savage choric function is concluded at the very moment when he could have become an even more significant moral guide for the audience; Overdo, already distanced from their plane of the theatrical experience, is also morally compromised.

Once he has the licence, Quarlous even feels the need to justify his employment of a cutpurse to the audience (IV, vi, 25–8), especially when Edgworth invites him in to meet Ursla's prostitutes (IV, vi, 16–18). He excuses himself with a Latin tag (ll. 25–6), making him sound like Overdo. Soon he is in disguise like Overdo as well, stealing the clothes of the madman Troubleall, in order to find out who has been successful in winning Grace – the agreement was that a stranger would put a mark against the pseudonym of either of them in Grace's notebook. As soon as he discovers he has lost, however, Dame Purecraft offers herself to him, and reveals her own involvement in corrupt marriage dealings amongst the Puritans (V, ii, 44–62). 'Stand aside. I'll answer you presently' is Quarlous's response to her (l. 66). There follows a monologue in which he persuades himself that there is no reason why he should not have both Dame Purecraft and her portion: 'why should I not marry the money when 'tis offered me?' (ll. 71–2). In the 1631 Folio text Jonson prints the remarkable stage direction '*He considers with himself of it*' against this speech. Such marginal commentary is not unusual in the 1631 text, and is often used to describe the character's actions rather than indicating where a stage move might occur. (The speech concludes with the marginal direction in the Folio '*he takes her along with him*' (i.e. persuades her.) Here '*He considers with himself of it*' strongly suggests that the actor playing Quarlous does not speak this speech to the audience, but to himself – as it seems Overdo has done on similar occasions when he has had a decision to make or a plan to work out (III, iii, 1–35; V, i, 1–8), speeches which would conventionally be soliloquies spoken to the audience. Quarlous has now acquired the relationship – or rather lack of it – with the audience which marked out Overdo's position as choric judge in the play. No one is left to talk critically to the audience.

It is entirely fitting then that when Adam Overdo stages what he thinks is his triumphant moment of judgement, removing his disguise and bringing down censure upon the heads of the transgressors, he is upstaged by Quarlous. Quarlous reveals the justice's foolish bias which made him unable to see that Edgworth was not a virtuous young gentleman, and shows how he has won both Dame Purecraft and, thanks to a deception which he practised on Overdo whilst disguised as Troubleall (V, ii, 86–112), the guardianship of Grace. Winwife has her hand, but only at the cost of her losing her wealth to Quarlous. But if Overdo seemed to want to play the role of the Avocatori in *Volpone*, and Quarlous to be a mixture of Dauphine in *Epicoene* and Lovewit in *The Alchemist*, there is no rancour at the end of this play. Overdo immediately agrees to Quarlous's suggestion that they should all repair to the Justice's house 'and drown the memory of all enormity in your biggest bowl at home' (V, vi, 91–2).

The play allows no one, ultimately, to stand aside from the fair and remain unaffected by it, and permits no one to communicate with the audience in a position of mutual understanding which is devoid of dramatic irony. The simplistic moralising of Overdo was refused this position from the start, and the reason for this was revealed by Dame Purecraft. The cynical, snobbish misogyny of Quarlous may well have initially amused the audience (or parts of it), but could not be sustained in the face of the temptations on offer within the world-of-the-play. Ultimately the play turns in on itself, as the characters all focus on the onstage puppet performance, a show whose conclusion takes place offstage, in the world-in-the-play, it would seem ('We'll ha' the rest of the play at home'; V, vi, 104–5). Whether carnival or market, or both, the whirlpool of the fair sucks into its embrace the would-be critic.

The genial ending of the play, even if it invites meta-theatrical speculation (see above, p. 124), leaves no moral challenge for the audience. In fact it jovially and fantastically turns its back on them. *Bartholomew Fair* is formally a brilliant reworking of the methods of the earlier Jacobean plays, but concludes by looking forward to the later, much more theatrically conventional Caroline romantic comedies.

CRITICAL APPROACHES

Mikhail Bakhtin's influential account of the significance of carnival festivity in early modern culture has often been seen to provide a useful critical approach to *Bartholomew Fair* (Bakhtin 1968). 'In Bakhtin's "festive marketplace" ', writes Jonathan Haynes,

> There is a 'temporary suspension, both ideal and real, of hierarchical rank', preserving utopian memories of a primitive communism. All exchanges are between equals, and are frank and free, as is language, often to the point of obscenity and abuse. The physical body is reviled and celebrated; the air is full of universal laughter.
>
> (Haynes 1992: 120)

This might well seem to express the fair's nature, where preacher and magistrate are both humbled, gentlewomen are willingly led astray and the foul-mouthed and fleshy Ursla literally holds centre stage (Jonson 1963: 210), dispensing ale and pork amidst whores and low-lifes.

Peter Womack finds this an apt model, and writes that Lent never comes to the carnival of *Bartholomew Fair* (Womack 1986: 147). He observes that what structures the play is the consciousness of the respectable visitors, who are all related by permanent legal bonds such as marriage or service. The atomised fair people, on the other hand, who are only inter-related by temporary business dealing of one sort or another, provide the background to the story of their visitors: 'the Fair people are, roughly speaking, what happens to their visitors' (Womack 1986: 148). Yet as the play progresses the bonds which unite the visitors are dissolved in the fair, and the subordinate, fragmented consciousness overwhelms 'the legal and domestic one; the context, so to speak, swamps the text. It's this profound structural joke which produces the impression that the play is sprawling and episodic' (Womack 1986: 149).

Furthermore, there is no unified time scheme which can be plotted through the text. Womack shows through a close analysis of the second half of the play that there is 'no authoritative "day" to which all the separated trajectories of the characters conform . . . but a ramshackle ensemble of different times that chime only when people become involved in the same scene' (Womack 1986: 152–3). The impossible (in naturalistic terms) closeness of the different booths on stage violates the conventional representation of space on stage. Thus there is no one unified dramatic consciousness representing the world, and the unities of time and place parody themselves 'and subvert the ideal of naturalness from within' (Womack 1986: 154). Womack considers that Jonson's other middle comedies struggle to reconcile the contradiction involved in showing the real world by false, theatrical, means. But:

> in *Bartholomew Fair* . . . that rift is mended because the depicted world is itself a show . . . in the sense that in the Fair's estranging network of intercutting personal trajectories, everyone *is* such an exhibit for everyone else. Everyone is detached from the institutional fixities which guarantee his 'real self'; every identity is made over to the transformative

fluidity of the crowd . . . the performance itself resembles
what it denotes.

(Womack 1986: 155)

Bartholomew Fair puts carnival on stage because it 'reproduces its
fundamental condition: that the subject of the discourse is collective,
neither an official nor a deviant individual but the whole body of the
people' (Womack 1986: 157). This is not the representation of a
fictional world, but play, a game, in which the audience also partici-
pated, as is acknowledged in what Womack calls the 'spoof' indenture in the Induction. Just as in a court masque, a text written for a
single performance which relied upon the spectators joining in the
dance to complete the action, this is a text 'which reaches out for
its completion to the real presence in which it is performed'.
Bartholomew Fair is Jonson's 'masque for the people' (Womack 1986:
159). This is not, however, the same kind of temporal effect which I
identified in *The Alchemist*, where the identity of onstage and offstage
time (see above, pp. 101–2) effaced representation to produce ludic
theatre. Womack suggests that the parodying of the unity of time
produces an estrangement effect which invites knowing audience
engagement with the play's festive, carnivalesque agenda.

Jonathan Haynes is less optimistic, and notes that Bakhtin insists
that festivity was 'a mode of social expression and organization',
and as such subject to social change (Haynes 1992: 119). He sees
Bartholomew Fair as Jonson's account of the disintegration of carnival before the scrutiny of church, state and, in particular, the capitalist market. The carnivalesque guiltless enjoyment of bodily
pleasures and the community of equals is not, he argues, eventually
enjoyed by all in the play, but only by those who are represented as
underworld figures: Ursla, Knockem, Edgworth, Whit, Punk Alice
and the others. The hierarchy among the respectable visitors is not
dissolved by the fair; rather the fair becomes a background against
which the moral status of the bourgeois characters is revealed to be
not consonant with their social position. In the same way Grace and
Winwife's courtship and marriage is made possible by the fair, but
neither participates in it. Haynes notes that almost the first line
Grace speaks is in scorn of the Fair (I, v, 134–6): 'she is carried along
anyway, but her icy reserve is never broken' (Haynes 1992: 126).

As for Quarlous, Haynes writes that, although Grace and Winwife merely profit from the social opportunity which the distraction of the others at the fair provides, 'Quarlous has the virtues – alertness, aggressiveness, the ability to improvise, a detached but practical intelligence, and a willingness to get his hands dirty – that make one master in this world' (Haynes 1992: 129). Quarlous sees that the modern market place is for accumulation, not festivity. When he adopts the disguise as Troubleall (IV, vi, 138–9), he shows 'that he knows how to manipulate the symbol system of the fair without believing in it himself' (Haynes 1992: 128). Jonson observes that in Jacobean London, the day of carnival is over: 'the suspension of normal social relations leads not to primitive equality, or to a pristine and ideal social order, but to an acceleration of the processes of social Darwinism' (Haynes 1992: 129). The audience do not participate in the experience of the fair in any sense, but an alienating Induction ensures that they remain detached and sitting in judgement. Haynes cannot believe that the dinner at Justice Overdo's (V, vi, 101) will be a genuine, egalitarian festivity: 'can Grace really sit down with Ursla? How will Winwife get along with Quarlous . . . ? . . . Real social festivity has become a utopian idea . . . a purely symbolic event' (Haynes 1992: 138).

Jonson's own ambivalence about the fair is proposed by critics who are convinced of the playwright's own latent antitheatricalism. Stallybrass and White see Jonson as engaged in a struggle to establish himself as the independent author of highstatus works of art whilst knowing fully that he is striving to make his living in a popular art form itself traditionally regarded as socially degraded. The act of writing a play about the fair was, for Jonson, an assertion that the theatre is not a fair: 'as much an act of dissociation from, as an engagement with, its festive space' (Stallybrass and White 1986: 61). At the centre of the play they see Ursla and her pig booth, symbolising moral corruption. Her own open, thirsty yet secreting female body not only undergoes a series of changes, 'but is the agent of transformation in others' (Stallybrass and White 1986: 65). No religious, educational or civil censor can overpower her: 'it is the language of the grotesque body which triumphs over the languages of the Scriptures and the classics' (Stallybrass and White 1986: 70). Against such subversion and filth Jonson establishes himself as the author, the royal authority which can present the degradation of popular festivity, contesting a space between aristocratic disdain and popular patronage yet only having the existing discourses to work in; he cannot escape the 'dirt' both of Smithfield, his subject matter, and of the contamination of the theatrical market place (Stallybrass and White 1986: 65). In her re-evaluation of her earlier thoughts on the play, Leah Marcus detects in the play's framing devices not only a characteristic defence against uncongenial modes of interpretation, but also 'the language of Jacobean anti-theatricality': 'futile attempts at containing his own ludic impulses along with the populist energies he purported to despise' (Marcus 1995: 177).

Some critics have noted a Christian structure underlying the play's plot. David Riggs sees Adam Overdo as the Christ figure, 'who descends from on high, adopts the form of lowly man, preaches a sermon to the multitudes and is persecuted and physically beaten' (Riggs 1989: 212). Later he returns in judgement, when he will 'break out in rain, and hail, lightning and thunder upon the head of enormity' (V, ii, 4–5). But Quarlous recognises 'the formal structure of the allegory' and exploits it so that he gains Grace's wealth, a parody of divine grace. Riggs writes that Jonson has, in the same way, treated 'the biblical narrative of the mystery cycles as a manipulable fiction' to be exploited (Riggs 1989: 213), and speculates that this was the blasphemous attitude to scripture which the biographer Aubrey said Jonson later regretted (HSS I: 181). Jackson Cope reads the biblical narrative differently. He sees Adam Overdo as an Old Testament Jehovah figure who by the end of the play has 'learned mercy only through his discovery of the weakness in a human cosmos' (Cope 1984: 90). Troubleall takes on more of the Christ role, as the ragged prophet who calls for mercy and love, with his cry of 'quit ye, and multiply ye' (IV, i, 97). If there is apparent blasphemy against God's omnipotence, however, Cope sees the union of Winwife and Grace an allegory of the incarnation, 'a concord of flesh and blood living together to multiply in the mysterious, even mad destiny of their union of love' (Cope 1984: 90).

Kristen McDermott finds the union of Grace and Winwife far from mysterious. Rather, 'she emerges as a realistic young woman who deals with her very real predicament in an unconventional way, and simultaneously as a symbol in the sense that her transformations as a woman reflect the transformations Jonson sees in contemporary morality' (McDermott 1993: 108). McDermott sees Grace's self-control as unappealing, and notes her masculine-sounding language and her unemotional and business-like declaration of love to Winwife (V, ii, 27–33). Grace's self-sufficiency comes from her recognition that she is a commodity, and that she can have some agency in this world if she shapes her own destiny by making herself 'a new product designed for the narrow and specialized market represented by Quarlous and Winwife' (McDermott 1993: 108).

In general the fair, a place where in the past the subversive potential of female sexuality may have been active, is shown in the play to succumb 'to the pressures of the marketplace' (McDermott 1993: 93). The pregnant Win, for example, is objectified and offered out by her husband in the first act (I, ii, 2–14; see also Miller 1996: 92–3). Once in the fair, consumption for its own sake – excess – transforms her wholesome fertility and what was intimate becomes public. 'The moment she enters the fair', writes McDermott, 'Win becomes vulnerable to the forms of chaos brought on by sexual incontinence (cuckoldry) and by incontinent eating and drinking (inappropriate urination and nausea)' (McDermott 1993: 99). Win's need to urinate (III, vi, 11–12) indicates that her body is no longer closed and contained as a chaste woman's should be. She has to re-enter Ursla's pig booth, where her foolish husband leaves her to see to his puppets. There Knockem blazons her as a horse for sale (IV, v, 17–24), and she is drunkenly persuaded to take on the costume and the life of a whore: 'the mask and the green gown of the prostitute, like a player's costume, is transforming to the point that Win almost seems turned inside out' (McDermott 1993: 101). She concludes:

As London's urban spread and urban *mores* have entrapped and encroached upon the Fair, so have the pressures of urban life and morals encroached on the creative aspect of female desire, turning modest mothers into whores, honest whores into impoverished cripples [Ursla], and the infinite bounty of divine grace into a commodity cynically negotiated by money-hunting, sex-fearing men.

(McDermott 1993: 115)

THE PLAY IN PERFORMANCE

There is no record that *Bartholomew Fair* was performed in Jonson's lifetime after 1 November 1614, but the play became an immediate favourite at the Restoration when its satire on Puritanism seemed to make it popular with Charles II (Noyes 1935: 228–9).[8] In 1690 Thomas D'Urfey published a comic poem, *Collin's Walk Through London and Westminster*, in which the ignorant countryman Collin is taken to the theatre where *Bartholomew Fair* is playing. Mistaking it for a religious meeting, when Busy is placed in the stocks (III, vi, 97), Collin invades the stage, sword in hand, to release him. The audience are delighted (reproduced in Noyes 1935: 231–3). Noyes remarks that Collin's actions are 'an implicit tribute to the excellence of playing at this performance', but D'Urfey's fiction rather acknowledges the play's self-conscious concern with how an audience should respond to its performance.

It is all the more surprising, then, that since the play's first full professional revival in 1950 the Induction has generally been dispensed with.[9] Michael Bogdanov's production at the Young Vic in 1978 replaced it as follows: 'Lantern Leatherhead came out, welcomed the audience to the Young Vic and ripped up a copy of the play, warning any culture-seekers that they would not want that rubbish' (Teague 1985: 132). In the second half of the twentieth century the play enjoyed a new lease of life as a theatrical vehicle for engaging with class conflict in a turbulent era in British politics, perhaps identifying the play's critique of emergent capitalism noted by some critics (see above, pp. 133–4, 135–6). But rather than foreground the audience's role as judging participants in the shared game of the drama, Bogdanov sought to position the audience as visitors to the fair themselves by 'using strips of cloth to make the entire theatre resemble a circus tent, as well as preshow action (arm wrestling, music, acrobats) in the foyer of the theatre and the street in front of it' (Teague 1985: 133). In a rival London production that same summer at the Round House Thelma Holt and Peter Barnes produced the same effect on a larger scale. Their impressive fairground outside the theatre featured a menagerie of animals, including Lucille and Heidi, the fortune-telling pigs. Inside the auditorium backless wooden benches replaced the seating for this three-hour play (Teague 1985: 134–5).

Both productions wanted the audience to share the experience of visiting the fair, where middle-class hypocrisy and corruption become exposed in the face of the temptations of a life more fully lived in the fairground. Bogdanov's production was in modern dress, interpolated with punk songs. Barnes's more genial production was in Jacobean costume, but with nineteenth-century fairground equipment, staged very nearly in the round. To read the play as a parable about class seems simplistic, given, for example, how Jonson creates Quarlous's relationship with the audience (see above, p. 129); to imagine that an audience will ever feel 'part of the fair' on stage also seems a superficial idea, especially in the face of Jonson's complex negotiation of the relationship between performer and audience in this play.

Subsequent major productions have put more faith in the text itself and have not sought to impose a narrow political reading. Richard Eyre at the National Theatre in 1988 set the action in late Victorian London. Julie Sanders felt that in making this transposition he was 'cutting the dense topicality of the Jonsonian text and eschewing its central politics' (Sanders 1998a: 206 n. 24), but for one reviewer the production was a revelation. Irving Wardle in *The Times* (22 October 1988) saw for the first time that '*Bartholomew Fair* is as craftily constructed as *Volpone* and *The Alchemist.*' Moreover, 'for once a production has got on top of Jonson's language instead of being buried by it.' The hypocrisy of the 'elephantine, stone-faced' Busy (Jonathan Burke) was stressed not only by the fact that at his first entrance he 'rolls into view, having been detached with difficulty from a turkey pie', but also in his final confrontation with puppet Dionysus, 'when he loses his religious breeches, disclosing a frilly salmon-pink foundation garment'. There was a genuine conflict here between 'people who get on with their lives, and judges who try to control them'. An increasingly comic Overdo (John Wells) became steadily more ridiculous, 'a disapproving outsider irresistibly sucked into the life of the fair'. He did address the audience, as all modern Overdos seems to have done. But this was not a dark and cynical production, like Bogdanov's or Terry Hands's 1969 RSC version at the Aldwych in

1969 (see Jensen 1985: 48–52; Teague 1985: 124–8). Richard Cave thought that the extravagant Victorian fairground setting by William Dudley was a 'child's paradise of twinkling lights and whirling carousels . . . that tempts the starchy citizens to adopt a childish recklessness and irresponsibility that steadily give place to total abandon. The shift to deeper levels of humour was meticulously effected' (Cave 1991: 175–6 n. 3). Though affecting and very funny, this was, it seems, nevertheless a spectacle for a detached audience. No modern production has been prepared to take on the challenge implied in the Induction.

Eyre made full use of the huge Olivier stage for the fair. The intimacy afforded by the Swan and subsequently the Young Vic in London offered director Laurence Boswell for the RSC in 1997–9 greater opportunities for closer audience engagement. This *Bartholomew Fair* drew on that contemporary late August celebration of London life, the Notting Hill Carnival, for its inspiration, eclectic design and musical punctuation. The production certainly delighted, with fine, if occasionally over-excited ensemble playing. It was also expertly paced, allowing the carefully structured inventiveness and variety of the play's action to emerge in a very satisfying way. The text came through abridged, but fresh and unmodernised. Benedict Nightingale in *The Times* (26 February 1999) admitted that the cast 'catch the comic munificence, the exuberance and the subversive glee that made Jonson Jonson'. The edge of moral judgement and the challenge of meta-theatrical awareness were lacking, however. In this production John Quayle's Overdo became the star of the show, a genial old buffer who was our bemused guide to the action. David Henry's Busy was a loud, large, slobbering buffoon. It was very funny and humane, but there was something lacking. As Sarah Hemming wrote in her *Financial Times* review (2 March 1999), 'here the priest has no serious power and the judge no estimable wrath, so Jonson's scathing mockery of them loses its edge and the production doesn't seem to have a centre.' The Induction was, again, cut. What reflection there was on our own relationship to the action was limited to that induced by ultra-contemporary features of the design in a Jacobean play: the replica football shirts and the fashionable way of drinking beer from a bottle. The play awaits a modern revival which fully addresses the text's meta-theatrical requirements.

NOTES

1. It is possible that Overdo is also a depiction of some of the weaknesses of James himself; see Marcus 1986: 55–6.
2. The pulling down of the Market Cross at Banbury in 1600 and some acts of zealous magistracy uncannily echo some of play's language, writes Collinson (1995: 161–3). On the depiction of Puritanism in *Bartholomew Fair* and *The Alchemist* see also Lake 2002: 583–610.
3. Protestants regarded Catholic veneration of statues and relics as little different to the worship of pagan gods condemned in the Old Testament.
4. For an account of the play's 'engagement with questions of absolutism, limited monarchy and democracy' (p. 103) see Sanders 1998a: 89–104.
5. Gossett in Jonson (2000a: 103) marks Overdo's long speech '[*in soliloquy*]', which would imply that he is addressing the audience. But Hibbard in Jonson (1977: 79) does not mark the speech as soliloquy or aside, nor do HSS (VI: 66); nor, they suggest, does Gifford.
6. See Gurr 1992: 103; Escolme 2005: 6–11. Escolme writes of the early modern stage that 'in performance, these dramatic texts are dependent for their effects of subjectivity upon the potential for direct encounter between performer and spectator within a continually foregrounded theatre building' (p. 8).
7. Cope 1984: 88–9 goes so far as to compare him to Satan.
8. Riggs (1989: 213–14) suggests that the King's displeasure at the play's implied criticism of the King's own conduct in the Overbury case and elsewhere led to the play's neglect and subsequent failure to appear in print until 1631. Jonson wrote an 'Apology' for the play, now lost; its content is entirely unknown.
9. George Devine's production at the Edinburgh Festival and subsequently at the Old Vic was, apart from the Phoenix Society production of 1921, the first revival of Jonson's own text since 1731.

CHAPTER 8

The Devil is an Ass (1616)

Jonson's last play before a ten-year absence from the public stages was both a self-aware revisiting of the comedies since *Volpone* and an explicit departure from the moral project of those plays. Once again the Blackfriars was the venue.

CONTEXTS

In 1616 Jonson had achieved financial security, having been granted a royal pension. He had also established himself as a major literary figure with the publication of his *Works*. It seems as if *The Devil is an Ass*, which had its first performance in this year, offended someone important, but his status and the King's favour ensured that no further action would be taken against him – even though the play was withdrawn from the repertory at royal command (*Conv.*, l. 355).

Drummond's account seems to suggest that the cause of the play's suppression was its satire on 'projectors', as represented in the play by the character of Merecraft. Merecraft is a fraudster who persuades the improvident to invest money in spurious schemes, including implausible inventions which will be granted a royal monopoly (II, i, 41–109). Whether the satire was aimed at the King's favourite Sir Robert Carr, or the Earl of Argyle, or even at James's own interest in Alderman Cockayne's project (see Evans 1994: 62–77), it was clearly felt to have hit its target.

Jonson also chose to satirise the subject matter of popular 'devil plays' such as the anonymous *Merry Devil of Edmonton* (1602), which he mentions in the Prologue (l. 22), and Dekker's *If This be Not a Good Play, the Devil is in It* (1611). In these plays the devil arrives in a sophisticated, wicked world, where man proves to be more than the devil's match and outwits him. But in *The Devil is an Ass* Pug, the tyro devil sent down to earth with one last chance to prove himself to Satan, finds himself ignored and irrelevant to the machinations and deceptions of these amoral citizens of London.

As Satan recognises, it is historical change itself which has marginalised him. The devilry which would convince audiences in 1560 will not do now, when there are 'other things/ That are received on earth for Vices,/ Stranger and newer' (I, i, 100–2). Both the figure of the Iniquity and the doggerel couplets of up to fourteen syllables which he speaks are hopelessly out of date; he is presented with a kind of world-weary nostalgia. Jonson in this very funny scene shows a rejection of the static, medieval view of moral conflict as embodied in the diabolical figure. As James Loxley writes, 'it formulates an awareness of the breach between past and present that cultural historians have described as the archetypal experience of "modernity"' (Loxley 2002: 91). A 'modern' 'imaginatively engaged and vital dramatic tradition has to be a state of continual renewal', writes Richard Cave (1991: 128), and this play is nothing if not imaginatively engaged as it addresses its main concern: the act of representation itself (Loxley 2002: 90).

THE PLAY

Having taken on the body of a young cutpurse hanged that morning, Pug finds employment in the household of Fitzdottrel, a 'Squire of Norfolk', obsessed with trying to summon demons. Fitzdottrel will not believe Pug's protestations that he really has come from Satan (I, iii, 25–6), but takes him on because he likes his name, 'Devil'. There follows a remarkable scene (I, vi). Wittipol, a young gallant, wishes to seduce Fitzdottrel's young wife Frances, who is clearly unhappy in her marriage to an avaricious and foolish husband. Her husband agrees that Wittipol can address her in his presence for fifteen minutes, provided Wittipol does not touch her. In return Fitzdottrel can have Wittipol's cloak. All that matters to Fitzdottrel is that he can show off this expensive garment to the audience when he visits the theatre that afternoon. The play which he will see is *The Devil is an Ass*.

Anne Barton and Richard Cave consider that Jonson is satirising here those audience members who would be too self-obsessed to notice when the play addresses their own follies, even if they were to see themselves on stage (Cave 1991: 122; Barton 1984: 227). Jonson's obvious target would be the gallants in their rich clothes who sat on stools at the sides of the Blackfriars stage, getting in the actors' way, whom the Prologue had addressed (ll. 10–20). In my experience of modern performance, however, the impact on the audience of this announcement is meta-theatrical, not satirical. If the fictive, onstage representation of London of *The Devil is an Ass* is a different kind of world from the 'real' world of the audience,[1] and if Fitzdottrel is a character from that fictive world, at the Blackfriars he will, impossibly, have to be not only in two places at once but in two worlds at once. This is perhaps the boldest assertion in the middle comedies that the onstage and offstage worlds are to be understood as the same 'world', that Jonson's theatre is play, not illusion.

Almost as startling is the presence of Fitzdottrel's watch on stage counting down the fifteen minutes. Wittipol uses an argument familiar from love poetry in his attempted seduction. Youthful beauty does not last long and Frances should enjoy it while she can:

> Think,
> All beauty does last until the autumn.
> You grow old while I tell you this.
>
> (I, vi, 129–31)

It is a moment when we are aware that the actor playing Frances, and all of the audience too, are ageing in the same 'real' time. Our moral response to a scene where 'it is virtually impossible not to back the cause of adultery' (Barton 1984: 226) is affected by a moment where all of us in the theatre listen attentively to sensual language in acute awareness of our own physicality and mortality.

It is a remarkable moment. Peter Happé notes that everything in the play

> is subordinate to Jonson's sense that the stage is all artifice and trickery, and his skill in working with an audience in such a way that they know it is so, and yet can be induced to find a sharper sense of the real world.
>
> (Jonson 1996: 21)

Stage time and real time coincide here, as they did in *The Alchemist* (see pp. 101–2 above), but the passing of time is explicitly foregrounded to produce this moral impact on the audience.

Peter Womack reads this line differently. He argues that in *The Devil is an Ass* Jonson dramatises the shift from the emblematic representation of the morality play (see above, p. 14) to a 'secular theatre of illusion' (Womack 1986: 45) based on a psychologically convincing representation of character. But estrangement effects such as this, he suggests, tease the audience by showing the unnaturalness of 'naturalistic' theatrical illusion. For Womack it is significant overall that Pug cannot cope with illusion, which dominates the world of the play, a world where 'the people he meets never say what they mean' (Womack 1986: 44). But the deceitful social intercourse of Jacobean London is not illusion in the sense of stage 'illusion', as Womack suggests. 'Estrangement' is not a useful term in a theatre which requires little or no suspension of disbelief. Pug may be fooled by illusion but Jonson's audiences are under no pretences.

Frances sends an ambiguous message to Wittipol through Pug, and her would-be lover encounters her from a window close enough to her room for some physical intimacy (II, vi, 70 s.d.). Pug has already attempted to seduce Frances, in a clumsy attempt at wickedness. Mrs Fitzdottrel, thinking that this is a test of her fidelity set up by her husband, summoned her spouse to upbraid him, and Pug received a cudgelling. In revenge he informs Fitzdottrel of the meeting at the window and Wittipol flees. Thus Pug's desire to do evil only succeeds in doing 'good': forestalling adultery. The conventional moral categories of the morality play are in disarray.

The adultery plot has an unexpected conclusion, however, and for the first time since *Poetaster* in 1601 there is explicit, unambiguous moral instruction from the Jonsonian stage. Merecraft and his sidekick Engine have laid a plan which they hope will lead to Fitzdottrel giving them control over his estate. It entails him signing over his property to a third party to show his apparent earnest intent in advance of a potentially fatal duel. Frances has been sent to Lady Tailbush and her friends, where she is to learn how to behave in a manner appropriate to the status of the future Duchess of Drowned-land, which her husband believes she will attain. The paragon of ladylike behaviour at this soirée is one 'Spanish lady', a construction of Merecraft, who is actually Wittipol having donned the disguise to see more of Frances.[2] When Wittipol is eventually (apparently) alone with Frances, she appeals to the virtue she had seen in him earlier and asks him to be the friend she needs to save her from destitution, 'matched' as she is,

> to a mass of folly
> That everyday makes haste to his own ruin;
> The wealthy portion that I bought him, spent.
>
> (IV, vi, 20–2)

Wittipol agrees to become her selfless friend and to renounce the claims of a lover. It turns out that Fitzdottrel has become enamoured of the 'Spanish lady' and in that disguise Wittipol persuades him to grant the deed of 'feoffment', granting control over Fitzdottrel's property, to Fitzdottrel's close friend Manly, who had witnessed the last encounter with Frances. When the deed is signed Wittipol reveals himself, then triumphantly 'baffles' Fitzdottrel (IV, vii, 73 s.d.).

To some critics this is a disappointing anti-climax. The straight-forwardly moral ending is unsatisfactory because it 'short-circuits dramatically the currents of excitement which its [the play's] best moments make us feel', writes Duncan (1979: 228). Womack does not find this moment 'convincing' because it suddenly transforms what he takes to be a psychologically realistic encounter between two 'characters' into an '*argument* between desire and prudence, trans-gressive and conformable love which is not natural but estrangingly discursive' (his italics) (Womack 1986: 47). There are still some traces of Jonsonian moral challenge and complexity, however. The marital difficulties of the Fitzdottrels are unresolved, and Wittipol's 'moral' victory has only been achieved by crooked means (Leggatt 1981: 147–8; Jonson 1996: 6). Merecraft and Engine remain unpunished at the end of the play. Overall, however, there is no irony in the moral message of the play's final speech, where Manly reminds the audience that we must recognise our own wrongdoing and feel shame. The plague is never far away (V, viii, 169–74).

Perhaps Jonson, about to abandon writing for the stage, had lost faith in his audience's ability to respond to the complex moral challenges posed by *The Alchemist* or *Volpone*; perhaps he was pessimistic about the corrupt and money-driven culture he saw around him in 1616 (Jonson 1996: 12; Riggs 1989: 241–2).

Richard Cave still finds the ending exciting. Satan's description of the inhabitants of London is one that could well be applied to the protagonists of the middle comedies in general: 'They have their Vices there, most like to Virtues; / You cannot know 'em apart by any difference' (I, i, 121–2). Wittipol's action challenges the audience's expectations about conventional romantic comedy. His 'uncasing', which takes place with an entire act still to follow, takes him out of the conventions and moral codes of the world of the play: 'now he has no place there and our perspective on that world has changed in consequence' (Cave 1991: 135). He only reappears as an observer of the frantic events of the play's closing minutes, having learned his moral lesson. His new status is announced by his first line in the final scene: 'How now, what play ha' we here?' (V, viii, 39). The other observers, the audience, are encouraged by his example to leave the play similarly affected.

CRITICAL APPROACHES

A sympathetic portrayal of the lot of intelligent women seems to be a feature of the play. Frances Fitzdottrel is 'the first woman in a Jonson comedy who can fairly be described as a heroine. She is young, beautiful, resourceful and intelligent, passionate but chaste' (Barton 1984: 224) – not unlike a Shakespearean heroine, in fact. She can be seen to be more than that. In her conduct and the response of Wittipol to her situation can be seen, according to Sanders, a 'suggestion of better ways to live in the here and now of

1616: a way that includes empathy for the female condition, respect for communities, and equality before the law and between the sexes' (Sanders 1998a: 119). Helen Ostovich points out that Frances is trapped in marriage to an idiot in a society where a wife's rights were negligble, even over the portion she brought to the union. Frances has a 'quest for agency and equality', but the play shows that 'women are victims of contradictory binary reasoning' (Ostovich 1999b: 171). The only options available to her are a legitimate relationship with Fitzdottrel, or to be identified, as an adulteress, with the coarse and adulterous Lady Tailbush.

Ostovich, drawing on a likely source for the Wittipol plot, the story of Pyrocles and Zelmane in Sir Philip Sidney's *The New Arcadia*, shows that Wittipol shares something of what it is like to be Frances. In the seduction scene he took on her voice to give answer, since she cannot speak herself (I, vi, 154–92). He shares her helplessness when her husband strikes her at the window scene (II, vii, 16). Furthermore, 'his impersonation of the Spanish Lady moves him away from the inversions of Jonson's London, where men and women become equals in baseness, and instead lets him experience the alternative gender theorized by the Sidney family' (Ostovich 1999b: 172). She refers here not only to *The New Arcadia*, where Pyrocles, through playing the role of a woman in order to be nearer his lover, comes to see the same capacity for virtue in men and women, but to the example of a member of the Sidney family, Lady Mary Wroth, the poet who was a close friend of Jonson and to whom he dedicated *The Alchemist*. Her personal situation can be seen to have similarities to that of Frances Fitzdottrel (Ostovich 1999b: 156–64). When Wittipol promises that he can love 'Frances's "goodness" even more than her beauty, he crosses the threshold into to de-gendered friendship that recognises her right to an independent existence and goals that have nothing to do with him' (Ostovich 1999a: 174). Manly, in speaking the play's moralising final speech, endorses the underlying feminism of the play's presentation of the lot of married women when he insists that Frances has 'equal right' to her husband's land (V, viii, 165).

Widows in Jacobean England could enjoy a freedom denied to their married sisters. In the play's final scene, Fitzdottrel takes to his bed in feigned madness in an attempt to invalidate the signing over of the feoffment to Manly. Ostovich finds a positive ending to the play here. Fitzdottrel

> looks sick, feels sick, and is deemed sick and worthless by others. The final version of the bedridden husband, surrounded by not exactly well-wishing survivors of his schemes, strongly favours the idea of Fitzdottrel as virtually dead and incapable of resurrection. Pseudo-widowhood is Frances's happy ending.
>
> (Ostovich 1999b: 177)

The Devil is an Ass has been seen as something of a weak coda to the great middle comedies. It fails, according to Kay, to 'raise Jonson's comedy to new heights' (Kay 1995: 152). Jonson recycles material from the other middle comedies, such as the Spanish disguise from *The Alchemist*, the feigned madness from *Volpone* and the deed giving control over a lady's estate from *Bartholomew Fair*. Richard Cave defends the play by suggesting that the self-references make the play 'an apology for his own style of comedy', as he seeks to invest what are in danger perhaps of becoming the conventions of Jonsonian comic form and practice with an invigorating immediacy' (Cave 1991: 128). But Jonson's biographer David Riggs suggests that 'the overall effect is close to self-parody,' and that the retreat from moral challenge and ambivalence may be deliberate; perhaps this is Jonson renouncing his art, breaking his staff and retiring from the stage. There is an obvious echo of the epilogue of Shakespeare's *Tempest* (1611), which many have taken to be Shakespeare's farewell to the stage, in Manly's epilogue: 'Thus the projector is here overthrown./ But I have a project now of my own' (ll. 1–2).[3] It is certainly a farewell to Jonson's most exciting work. That he should end with a humane and sympathetic insight into the predicament of the wife in Jacobean society is both unexpected and intriguing.

THE PLAY IN PERFORMANCE

There is no convincing evidence that *The Devil is an Ass* was performed after 1616 until Peter Barnes adapted the play for the Nottingham Playhouse in 1972, and subsequently for the

Birmingham Repertory Company (1976–7) (Jonson 1996: 21–6). Matthew Warchus then directed a totally Jonsonian text for the RSC in Stratford and London in 1995–6.

Warchus's production was bold, pacy and spectacular. Hell was a garish nightmare of lurid fluorescent latex and booming voices. We saw the cutpurse hanged whose body Pug was to inhabit. It certainly undercut any expectations the audience may have had about 'conventional' Jonsonian comedy, as Lois Potter suggests (1999: 203). The explosion at Newgate which enabled Satan to rescue Pug and drag him back to Hell in Act V was startling and impressive.

Fittzdottrel (David Troughton) and Merecraft (John Nettles) emerged as two powerful stage creations. John Peter praised Troughton's 'agility and mulishness, Neanderthal cunning and stupidity' (*The Sunday Times*, 9 April 1995: 10); Benedict Nightingale thought his performance overcame the fact that Fitzdottrel's 'extreme gullibility is hard to credit' (*The Times*, 6 April 1995: 33). Peter thought Merecraft dangerous, 'a man about town who is elegant, self-possessed, plausible and alert' (*The Sunday Times*, 9 April 1995: 10). Peter Happé also noted the great theatricality of the pair, but found Merecraft 'to be not quite so irresistible as might have been expected: 'genial he may appear, but wicked he is' (Jonson 1996: ix). As for Fitzdottrel, Happé felt that behind the mania the character was 'a presence, rather than a butt . . . there was a distinctive human drive for individuality and integrity.' The final image of the play saw 'Fitzdottrel, still clutching the cross used in the hilariously comic exorcism, facing his wife across the bed which had been the site of so much comic misunderstanding' (Jonson 1996: vii).

The meta-theatricality of the cloak scene (I, vi) produced delighted laughter in the auditorium, as did the lines when 'Dougie' was substituted for 'Dick Robinson' in the scene where the actor who originally played Wittipol was described as inadequate to impersonate the Spanish lady (III, iv, 4–16 and n. 2).[4]

The scenes between Wittipol (Douglas Henshall) and Frances (Joanna Roth) were played with sensitivity, so that Wittipol's sudden conversion from lover to friend had genuine dramatic and emotional impact. The scenes following this moment in fact seemed rather anti-climactic, as the play rushed to its conclusion with pyrotechnics and grotesquery. The 'possessed' Fitzdottrel 'fakes levitation, spits out bits of factitious fire, drools shaving foam . . . and looks as if his head is about to twirl in circles' (*The Times*, 6 April 1995: 33). In fact John Peter felt that the production's pace and satirical energy were misdirected; the 'precise social background' of Jacobean money-making was lost. Dialogue which needed to be 'lethally articulated' was 'badly gabbled' (*The Sunday Times*, 10 April 1995: 10). Fitzdottrel and Merecraft are more complex and carefully drawn characters than Volpone and Face, and needed to be presented accordingly. Perhaps there is a greater 'realism', psychological and social, than in the plays which precede it.

All seemed to agree that there was an unexpected poignancy in the play: 'Warchus' production was at its best when . . . it evoked a sort of poetry from the confrontation of inadequate human beings with the infinite possibilities of human materialism' (Potter 1999: 203). This more sympathetic Jonson would be seen on the public stage again, but not for a decade.

NOTES

1. In *The Semiotics of Theatre and Drama*, Keir Elam defines the stage as being a different 'world' to that of the audience; its characters are 'conventional projections' from our world who 'are clearly not in a position to conceive of our world . . . as a hypothetical alternative of their own' (Elam 1980: 109).
2. For further meta-theatrical games concerning the actor Dick Robinson as the original Wittipol, see Barton 1984: 228 and McEvoy 2004: 77–8.
3. Compare 'Now my charms are all o'erthrown,/ And what strength I have's mine own' (Epilogue, ll. 1–2). For a scandalous suggestion that Fitzdottrel's feigned madness may be a satirical application to Shakespeare's own recent deathbed, see Duncan-Jones 2001: 276–7.
4. Lois Potter felt that 'the joke was only apparent to the small number of spectators who had read their programme with care' (1999: 203), but in the performance I saw 'Dougie' was a so obviously un-Jacobean name as to have the desired effect on most spectators.

CHAPTER 9

The Late Plays (1626–34)

Although they were notoriously dismissed as 'dotages' by the poet and critic Dryden (HSS I: 278), recent criticism has sought to rehabilitate the plays which Jonson wrote after a ten-year break from the stage. Although Jonson's deliberate contribution to contemporary political debate in these four plays has now been recognised, the case for their theatrical effectiveness remains to be made.

CONTEXTS

The royal pension which Jonson was granted in 1616 (see above, p. 5) secured his financial independence. He could also depend upon commissions from King James for writing court masques. Although it is clear that Jonson had started work on *The Staple of News* before the King's death in March 1625, it was evident that he would not be able to rely on the new regime of Charles I for support with the same confidence. Jonson's return to the stage may have been dictated by a need to make a living.

The theatrical climate had of course changed since 1616. The plays of Beaumont and Fletcher and their imitators were dominant. Michael Hattaway notes that in 1630 half of the evening performances of the King's Men at both the court at the Cockpit Theatre (the successor to the Blackfriars) were of Beaumont and Fletcher dramas (Jonson 1984: 2). Hattaway describes Caroline drama's desire to imitate the manners and conversation of the court, and not to alienate rich city merchants. No attempt was made to examine politics or society, or even individual psychology in a searching way: 'instead of analysing the deep rifts that were appearing in the structures of English society, Caroline dramatists tended to ignore them' (Jonson 1984: 3). This was a stage agreeable to the court of the uxorious Charles I, a court which, unlike that of his father, fostered elegance and gentility; but it was not one on which Jonsonian drama could find a welcome.

Nor was it an atmosphere in which the 20-stone, hard-drinking playwright could feel at home. After a stroke in 1628 Jonson was bedridden. As Anne Barton (1984) has demonstrated, at the end of his life his plays look back nostalgically to the glory days of Elizabethan England and rework its genre of romantic comedy in a manner quite at odds with the sentiments of the middle comedies. Jonson died in August 1637 with a final play, *The Sad Shepherd*, unfinished.

THE STAPLE OF NEWS (1626) AND *THE NEW INN* (1629)

Jonson had dealt with the issue of the burgeoning market for published news in his 1620 masque *News from the New World Discovered in the Moon*. He employed material from that work in *The Staple of News* at the Blackfriars in 1626. The owner of the eponymous publishing house which has cornered the news market is Cymbal, one of the play's suitors for the allegorical figure of Aurelia Clara Pecunia, 'Golden Shining Money'. The play's protagonist and fellow suitor is one Pennyboy Junior, who as the play opens comes into his inheritance. Pecunia is under the guardianship of his skinflint uncle Pennyboy Senior. Canter,[1] the beggar who brought news of Junior's father's death, is welcome at the new heir's side despite the abuse he receives from the crowd of tradesmen and hangers-on who cling to the wealthy Pennyboy Junior. During Junior's visit to Pecunia's lodgings, their trip to the Staple and the final revel at the Mitre Tavern, Canter – who speaks the play's only asides – offers a moral commentary on the foolish actions of Junior and his accompanying 'jeerers', not least on their jargon-filled language (IV, iv, 37–75). When Junior proposes endowing a College of Canters, the exasperated beggar reveals himself to be Junior's father, not dead, but who had 'done this to try how you would use/ Pecunia when you had her' (IV, iv, 119–20). The father takes Pecunia off into his custody.

Thus far the narrative has followed the 'prodigal' narrative familiar in Jacobean citizen comedies such as the anonymous *The London Prodigal* (1604). But in Act V the spendthrift son sets a trap for his father's unscrupulous lawyer Picklock who had connived to gain the family's wealth for himself, reveals the attorney's dishonesty, and wins back both his father's favour and Pecunia.

Pecunia is effectively presented as a figure from a masque. She wishes to be in the possession of neither the prodigal nor the miser, but to be put to good use, by applying 'the golden mean' (V, vi, 64). The Stuart masque, writes Richard Cave, sought allegorically to define the state of the ideal ruler's mind. In this play Jonson fuses masque with City Comedy (see above, p. 53) to present that pragmatic state of mind required in the city: 'a shrewd detachment through which one can manipulate the ways prevailing in the world (one hopes) to good advantage' (Cave 1991: 152).

Another schematic feature of the play is the chorus of four Gossips who sit upon the stage and pass comment on its characters and actions as the drama progresses. They misjudge the action both artistically and morally. Schematically they stand for free, foolish gossip as against the printed, commercial gossip of the Staple which seems to be of equivalent value. The 'golden mean' here is the theatre or perhaps the published play, commercial but virtuous in its desire for the reformation of morals. The presence on stage of the Gossips, however, as Don E. Wayne points out, shows that Jonson was so unconfident of his audience's response that he had to provide an explicit parody of how not to interpret the play as guidance. The commercial conditions of the Caroline theatre now undermine Jonson's humanist project of reform by the scholar-poet. The Gossips 'reflect the degree to which Caroline audiences and readers of play texts were beginning to take on an active and demanding role as consumers in establishing the canons of taste in the theater' (Wayne 1999: 81). Wayne also argues that the worship of Pecunia by parodies of courtly love and the masque in Acts III and IV turn the Jeerers, in the words of Pennyboy Canter, into 'engines . . . Mere monsters' (IV, ii, 136, 139). Thus 'Jonsonian drama represents an early registering of the deformation of social energy that occurs' when 'commodity exchange [i.e. Pecunia] comes to dominate social relationships and when the circulation of social energy is expressed as the circulation of money' (Wayne 1999: 74).

The Staple of News had a Blackfriars and a court performance in February 1626. The only recorded revival was a university production in New Zealand in 1973. This is not surprising. The play is an unsuccessful hybrid of masque and City Comedy. The first four acts are individual set pieces with little connecting plot to speak of. The linguistic display fails to take off in any of them. Jonson loses interest in the Staple itself which melts away, it is suddenly announced (V, i, 40–50). Above all, this is indeed a play 'where Jonson tells us what to think . . . eschewing the dense ironies and conflicting perspectives' of his earlier work (Jonson 1984: 32–3). In none of the late plays does Jonson attempt the bold representational strategies which made the middle comedies so challenging.

This is also true of *The New Inn*, even though it is a very theatrically self-conscious play. The Light Heart in Barnet is the play's setting, an inn on the road north of London. Goodstock is the host and he compares his guests to the characters of a play who pass across his stage (I, iii, 128–36; I, iii, 132–3).[2] On this day a new crowd appears at the inn whose mood is in distinct contrast to that of his melancholy guest Lovel. Lady Frances Frampul and her diverse entourage hold, for sport, a 'Court of Love', presided over by her witty chambermaid, Pru. The source of Lovel's sadness turns out to be his love for Lady Frances Frampul, a love he cannot declare because she is courted by Beaufort, a young lord whose care was entrusted to Lovel by Beaufort's noble father. Pru, who is aware of Lovel's feelings, allows him to speak in the Parliament for an hour first on the nature of love, and then for another hour about valour. His reward will be a kiss from Lady Frampul. Lovel's eloquence wins over Lady Frampul, but without either realising the other's feelings at the time. There follows a 'catastrophe' implausible even by the standards of Shakespearean romance. Beaufort, who has in fact fallen in love with Goodstock's young son Frank, disguised as a woman ('Laetitia') for a jest, marries 'him' only for his 'true' sex to be apparently revealed. At this point the old 'Irish nurse' pulls off her eye patch and reveals herself to be the mother both of Frances and of 'Frank', who really does have the name Laetitia. Beaufort's marriage is valid after all. The nurse is actually the older Lady Frampul who had 'left her home melancholic and jealous that her lord loved her not, because she had brought him none but daughters, and lives, unknown to her husband as he to her' ('The Persons', ll. 23–6). Goodstock then reveals himself to be her husband Lord Frampul. They are reconciled. Lovel will marry Frances. Pru is given a large dowry and will marry Beaufort's friend Latimer.

Such an ending invites the response that Jonson has either lost his touch or is awkwardly parodying romance. It has been very plausibly argued, however, that in these last plays he is a 'beleaguered intellectual courageously rethinking his priorities and making the painful accommodations necessary for him to survive in the uncongenial Caroline environment' (Butler 1992: 166). This entails not only some kind of 'circumspect' (Butler 1992: 167) accommodation with the growing fashion for the discourse of platonic love at court, as favoured by the Queen, but also the favourable depiction of old aristocratic blood and values. Both of these are located in the figure of Lovel, whose language links him to Jonson's patron the Earl of Newcastle (Butler 1992: 168–9; Riggs 1989: 302). Butler suggests that the moment of the play's composition, in early 1629, was a time when, following the assassination of the King's hated favourite Buckingham, some rapprochement between the court and its critics was possible. The play's language, with its talk of '*magna carta*' (I, ii, 24), and a 'petition . . . of right' (II, vi, 58), echoes the language of the critics of the monarchy who were about to assemble in the last parliament before Charles's prolonged period of personal rule. But Pru, as monarch, turns out to be both conciliatory and insistent on her prerogative (II, vi, 105, 249). Jonson wants the King to triumph over his powerful opponents, argues Butler, and this leads him to advocate a new, non-confrontational aristocratic ideology in opposition to the brash absolutism which had been favoured by the *arriviste* Buckingham. Sanders, on the other hand, finds a more covert republican agenda in *The New Inn*. She finds Lovel learning to abandon his aristocratic hauteur. As the play progresses the host instructs him in 'the value of . . . interhierarchical community', symbolised in the wise rule of the chambermaid Pru, who puts down the foolish knight Sir Glorious Tipto who insists on rights based on birth not merit (II, vi, 43–5, 48–50; Sanders 1998a: 160–1).

Whatever Jonson's precise political views at this point, *The New Inn* shows a keen interest in the transformational powers of theatre without any radical exploration of theatrical representation itself. Barton considers that role-playing and pretence by the characters in the Court of Love is 'a way of uncovering the real nature of its participants' and is as such 'quintessentially Shakespearean' (Barton 1984: 269): Barton takes *The New Inn* to be Jonson's homage to Shakespeare's insight in his late plays that 'palpable but highly charged fiction [i.e. the ending] . . . gains strength from the very honesty of its admission that this is how we should all like the world to be, but know that it is not' (Barton 1984: 281). Richard Cave feels that Jonson is at his most compassionate in this play. The self-conscious theatricality of the final scene has considerable fragility. We can see that the implausible but satisfying fantasy ending depends upon so many slight accidents: 'the last act is at once an admission and a kind of ritual exorcism of all those elements of chance that set the permanence of felicity continually at risk' (Cave 1991: 169). As such Jonson reveals explicitly to us why we need the genre of comedy.

In *The New Inn* Jonson quotes himself. The uncovering of the newly-wed 'Laetitia' to be Frank, who is in turn Laetitia in disguise, recalls the moment in *Epicoene* when Morose's husband is revealed to be a boy (*SW*, V, iv, 174). The moment in *The New Inn* is playing with genre convention, however, not undermining the conditions of gender representation on- and offstage as in *Epicoene* (see above, p. 85). The timed speeches of Lovel in the Court of Love recall Wittipol's fifteen minutes with Frances Fitzdotterel in *The Devil is an Ass* (I, vi). In the later play, however, there is no attempt to make stage time and real time coincide in a way which startles the audience's moral awareness of the scene (see above, pp. 143–4). These moments in the theatre are but shadows of Jonson's previous achievements.

Advocates of the play's quality as a theatrical rival to Jonson's earlier work may find the reviews of the 1987 RSC revival – the only professional outing since 1629 – sobering reading. The language and array of topical reference are no more abstruse than *The Alchemist* or *Bartholomew Fair*, but even the play's most generous critics found the low comedy of the inn's servants 'incomprehensible . . . where the play falls apart'; 'its defects all but outweigh its merits'; it was felt that 'there's far more bemusement than amusement'; furthermore, 'this may be a rare gem for academics but it lacks any lasting lustre as good theatre.'[3] Only Michael Coveney in *The Financial Times* (12 November 1987) found it unequivocally to be 'a real treat'. Lovel's discourses on love and valour, Coveney thought, 'are among the finest things Jonson wrote, and Mr [John] Carlile's delivery of them is electrifying'. It is interesting that Coveney found the 'mellow' and 'golden' setting, where the Light Heart merged into the Swan's own woodwork, appropriate to the play's 'nostalgic, reflective vein'. Ironically, it was the play's dream of an impossibly distant idealised aristocracy which, according to Peter Womack, 'is now part of the dream life of an industrial society in decline'. Consequently '*The New Inn* goes over better, or at least more easily in 1987 than it apparently did in 1629' (Womack 1989: 170) when its reception was famously hostile (Jonson 1984: 7). Perhaps Jonson too looks back wistfully but ineffectually on the playwright he once was.

THE MAGNETIC LADY, OR HUMOURS RECONCILED (1632) AND A TALE OF A TUB (1634)

When *The New Inn* was printed in 1631 Jonson blamed both the actors and the audience for its failure. The King's Men 'never acted', but 'negligently play'd' the text to 'a hundred fastidious impertinents' (Jonson 1984: plate 1; *Dedication*, ll. 4–5). In *The Magnetic Lady* Jonson responded by returning to his didactic practice in *Every Man Out of His Humour*. He put a two-man chorus on stage, to be guided by his mouthpiece (see above, p. 26). In this play it is a boy, John Try-gust, who offers guidance on how a comedy should be received. John explains that the author, 'finding himself now near the close', has returned to the depiction of various humours; but now he seeks to reconcile rather than castigate them. Hence the play's subtitle.

The eponymous Lady Loadstone has drawn around her a cast of various characters for dinner, three of whom are suitors, declared or undeclared, of her richly endowed fourteen-year-old niece Placentia. The girl is mysteriously ill. When Captain Ironside, enraged at Sir Diaphanous Silkworm's unmanly drinking habits, breaks his glass in the knight's face, the ensuing rumpus causes Placentia unexpectedly to give birth, saving her suitors, including the knight, from an ignominious alliance. At the centre of the action is Compass, 'a scholar, mathematic' (*The Persons*, l. 8) and perfect judge of the characters around him. He overhears Lady Loadstone's garrulous 'she-Parasite' (l.2) Polish tell Placentia's nurse Keep that she exchanged her own baby, Pleasance, for Lady Loadstone's in the cradle, and thus the true niece's innocence remains unsullied. To protect her own daughter she conspires with the midwife, Chair, to pretend that no child was born; it was merely a fit 'of the mother' (hysteria). Compass defeats her plan, marries Pleasance and extracts the niece's portion from the miserly Sir Moth Interest. Lady Loadstone and Ironside are paired off in marriage and the baby's father will marry Placentia. No one is punished, and those whose humours have clashed are indeed reconciled.

Whereas in *The New Inn* Jonson had shown a genuine interest in love, the pairings in *The Magnetic Lady* are as perfunctory as may be. The young women are not characterised at all, and the union of the soldier and the Lady is announced out of nothing. Compass emerges to a modern reader as a predatory opportunist in the matter of his marriage. Indeed, as Helen Ostovich has argued, 'what strikes a female audience of Jonson's play most insistently is the complete nullification of the woman's point of view' (Ostovich 1994: 440). The Jonson who had portrayed a young woman's plight so sympathetically in *The Devil is an Ass* (see above, pp. 146–7) now merely presents 'figures of male fantasy, to be contemplated and competed for' (Ostovich 1994: 425). The two young women are just two types of pleasure. Polish and Chair, the two older working-class women who attempt to appropriate childbirth and inheritance in their own interest are a threat to male dominance and are slapped down as Compass buys the support of the lawyer Practice to prove who is the true niece: 'the female controlled physical act has deviated into male-controlled economic and legal fact' (Ostovich 1994: 432).

Compass, like Macilente in *Every Man Out of His Humour*, represents the writer, but without the earlier play's ironic self-awareness. On the other hand, it can be argued that Compass's 'brother', the intelligent but violent and short-tempered Ironside, is a knowing self-portrait of the author (Barton 1984: 298–9). Both know their Jonson. Early in the play Compass gives an epigrammatic 'character' of Parson Palate in rhyming couplets. He admits that he is not the writer, but 'a great clerk/As any is of his bulk: Ben Jonson made it' (I, ii, 33–4). Jonson had put his name in the mouth of his characters before (*SW*, II, ii, 102), but without such explicit meta-theatricality. The effect, however, is of a character's self-conscious nod to his creator, merely an acknowledgement of the fictional status of the fantasy world of this implausible comedy of male wish-fulfilment. Nothing else in this awkward and rather brutal play touches on the potential moral power of the materiality of art in our lives.

A visitor to the bed-ridden Jonson in the early 1630s found him declaiming 'how mankind grew daily worse and worse,/ How God was disregarded' (Riggs 1989: 331). Jonson's last finished play, *A Tale of a Tub*, is full of good humour and optimism about human community, but it is set deliberately in what seem to be the early years of Elizabeth's reign or even slightly earlier (Barton 1984: 336: Butler 1992: 184). This jolly but unchallenging farce tells the story of the Valentine's Day marriage of Audrey Turf and of the five suitors for her hand on a rumbustious day of deceptions in a very rural Middlesex. All ends in harmony, and the cast settle down to watch In-and-In Medlay's masque, perhaps of shadow puppets, which retells the story of the day to its participants and ends with what seems to be a mirror image of the characters' dispositions on the stage. Whether the play is a challenge or an endorsement of the values of the Caroline court (Butler 1992: 179–85), Jonson's final concerns are to do with the relationship between art and life, and the moral and political possibilities inherent in that relationship.

The Magnetic Lady had three performances in 1632 (Riggs 1989: 334). There was a radio adaptation by Peter Barnes in 1987 and a student production at Reading University in 1996 (Jonson 2000b: 19). *A Tale of a Tub* was popular at the Cockpit Theatre, but not at court (HSS IX: 163); it has not been revived to my knowledge. In his final four plays Jonson seemed to have lost the confidence in his humanist project of reforming society through an exploration of the real presence of the represented theatrical world in our world. That project produced some of the funniest and most morally challenging dramas in the language, but it was over by 1626. The Jonson repertoire on the contemporary stage shows good judgement in its selection. If left to speak for themselves the great plays can still mix great profit with enormous pleasure.

NOTES

1. 'The word could also describe gypsies or other vagrant bands who used their own language or "canting" dialect' (Jonson 1984: 61).
2. In the 1987 RSC production the host left the stage at I, iii, 132 momentarily to watch the play from amongst the audience (Sanders 2003: 62–3).
3. Michael Billington in *The Guardian*, 12 November 1987; Francis King in the *Sunday Telegraph*, 15 November 1987; Peter Kemp in *The Independent*, 12 November 1987; Helen Rose in *Time Out*, 18 November 1987.

Further Reading

EDITIONS

At time of publication we still eagerly await *The Cambridge Edition of the Works of Ben Jonson*, edited by David Bevington, Martin Butler and Ian Donaldson, which will surely become the standard edition for Jonson scholars for many years to come. Wilkes remains the only recent available edition of all the plays in modern spelling. HSS remains a valuable collection of all Jonson's writing, supported by a wealth of commentary and contextual material. The Revels Series (Manchester University Press) contains most of Jonson's plays, many of which are also represented in the New Mermaids series (A & C Black/W W Norton).

CRITICAL STUDIES

Barton (1984) is a very influential and perceptive account of Jonson's career as a dramatist. Womack (1986) brings many of the insights of critical theory to the plays and is clearly influenced by the ideas of Bakhtin (see above, pp. 131–2). Haynes (1992) applies a historical, material criticism to the plays. Maus (1984) depicts a conservative Jonson motivated by the values of Roman Stoicism. Watson (1987) ingeniously suggests that Jonson's *œuvre* sought to contain and triumph over all other contemporary dramatic genres.

Donaldson (1997) is a series of wise and measured judgements about the meaning of the plays. Sanders (1998a) considers the presence of republican discourse in Jonson in the broadest sense. Loxley (2002) is an excellent guide to the criticism and is full of illuminating readings.

There are valuable collections of critical articles in Julie Sanders, Kate Chedgzoy and Susan Wiseman (1998a) (eds), *Refashioning Ben Jonson*, London: Macmillan; Martin Butler (1999) (ed.), *Representing Ben Jonson*, London: Macmillan; and Richard Dutton (2000) (ed.), *Longman Critical Readers: Ben Jonson*, Harlow: Pearson Education.

PERFORMANCE STUDIES

The performance history of the plays from after the Restoration until 1776 is detailed in Noyes (1935). Jensen (1985) picks up the story in the twentieth century. Cave (1991) is the first study of the plays from a fully theatrical perspective. The collection Richard Cave edited with Schafer and Woolland (1999a) is a rich source of opinions and ideas about Jonson on stage. Woolland (2003) traces the influence of Jonsonian theatre on the contemporary British stage.

CONTEXTS

Evans (1994) contains a series of detailed studies into the historical circumstances of the composition of several plays. A more general overview of the context can be found in Richard Harp and Stanley Stewart (2000) (eds), *The Cambridge Companion to Ben Jonson*, Cambridge: Cambridge University Press.

BIOGRAPHY

The standard work, despite its psychoanalytic approach, remains the excellent Riggs (1989). Kay (1995) locates each play very firmly in Jonson's social, artistic and political milieu.

Bibliography

Agnew, Jean Christophe (1986), *Worlds Apart: The Market and the Theater in Anglo-American Thought, 1550–1750*, Cambridge: Cambridge University Press.

Aristophanes (1964), *The Frogs and Other Plays*, trans. David Barratt, Harmondsworth: Penguin.

Aristotle (1965), *Poetics*, in *Classical Literary Criticism*, trans. T. S. Dorsch, Harmondsworth: Penguin.

Bakhtin, Mikhail (1968), *Rabelais and His World*, trans. Helene Iswolsky, Cambridge, MA: Harvard University Press.

Barbour, Richmond (1995), ' "When I Acted Young Antinous": Boy Actors and the Erotics of Jonsonian Theater', *Proceedings of the Modern Language Association*, 110, 1006–22.

Barish, Jonas A. (1956), 'Ovid, Juvenal and *The Silent Woman*', *Proceedings of the Modern Language Association*, 71, 213–24.

— (1960), *Ben Jonson and the Language of Prose Comedy*, Cambridge, MA: Harvard University Press.

— (1963), 'The Double Plot in *Volpone*', in Jonas A. Barish (ed.), *Ben Jonson: A Collection of Critical Essays*, Englewood Cliffs, NJ: Prentice Hall, pp. 93–105.

— (ed.) (1972), *'Volpone': A Casebook*, London: Macmillan.

— (1973a), 'Alchemy and Acting: The Major Plays of Ben Jonson', *Studies in the Literary Imagination*, 6, 1–22.

Barish, Jonas A. (1973b), 'Jonson and the Loathed Stage', in William Blissett, Julian Patrick and R. W. Van Fossen (eds), *A Celebration of Ben Jonson*, Toronto: Toronto University Press, pp. 30–46.

— (1981), *The Anti-theatrical Prejudice*, Berkeley, CA: University of California Press.

Barnes, Peter, Colin Blakely, Terry Hands and Irving Wardle (1972), 'Ben Jonson and the Modern Stage', *Gambit: International Theatre Review*, 6/22 , 5–30.

Barnes, Peter (1983), 'Staging Jonson', in Ian Donaldson (ed.), *Jonson and Shakespeare*, London: Macmillan, pp. 156–62.

Barton, Anne (1984), *Ben Jonson: Dramatist*, Cambridge: Cambridge University Press.

Benjamin, Walter (1970), 'The Work of Art in the Age of Mechanical Reproduction', in Hannah Arendt (ed.), *Illuminations*, London: Cape, pp. 211–44.

Bruster, Douglas (1992), *Drama and the Market in the Age of Shakespeare*, Cambridge: Cambridge University Press.

Butler, Martin (1992), 'Late Jonson', in Jonathan Hope and Gordon McMullan (eds), *The Politics of Tragicomedy*, London: Routledge, pp. 166–88.

Butler, Robert (2006), *'The Alchemist' Exposed*, London: Oberon.

Cartledge, Paul (1997), ' "Deep Plays": Theatre as Process in Greek Civic Life', in P. E. Easterling (ed.), *The Cambridge Companion to Greek Tragedy*, Cambridge: Cambridge University Press.

Cartwright, Kent (1999), *Theatre and Humanism: English Drama in the Sixteenth Century*, Cambridge: Cambridge University Press.

Cave, Richard (1991), *Ben Jonson*, London: Macmillan.

— (1999a), 'Visualising Jonson's Text', in Elizabeth Schafer and Brian Woolland (eds), *Ben Jonson and Theatre*, London: Routledge, pp. 33–44.

— (1999b), 'Acting in Jonson', in Elizabeth Schafer and Brian Woolland (eds), *Ben Jonson and Theatre*, London: Routledge, pp. 58–65.

— (2003), *'Poetaster*: Jonson and his Audience', in Brian Woolland (ed.), *Jonsonians: Living Traditions*, Aldershot: Ashgate, pp. 13–26.

Collinson, Patrick (1995), 'The Theatre Constructs Puritanism', in David L. Smith, Richard Strier and David Bevington (eds), *The

Theatrical City: Culture, Theatre and Politics in London, 1576–1649, Cambridge: Cambridge University Press, pp. 157–69.

Cope, Jackson I. (1984), *Dramaturgy of the Daemonic: Studies of Antigeneric Theater from Ruzante to Grimaldi*, Baltimore: Johns Hopkins Press.

Coryat, Thomas (2003), *Coryat's Crudities*, extract in Andrew Hadfield (ed.), *William Shakespeare's 'Othello': A Sourcebook*, London: Routledge, pp. 25–8.

Creaser, John (1994), 'Enigmatic Ben Jonson', in Michael Cordner, Peter Holland and John Kerrigan (eds), *English Comedy*, Cambridge: Cambridge University Press.

Danson, Lawrence (1984), 'Jonsonian Comedy and the Discovery of the Social Self', *Proceedings of the Modern Language Association*, 99, 179–93.

Di Gangi, Mario (1995), 'Asses and Wits: the Homoerotics of Mastery in Satiric Comedy', *English Literary Renaissance*, 25, 179–208.

Dollimore, Jonathan (2003), *Radical Tragedy*, 3rd edn, London: Palgrave.

Donaldson, Ian (1970), *The World Turned Upside-Down: Comedy from Jonson to Fielding*, Oxford: Clarendon.

— (1978), 'Language, Noise and Nonsense: *The Alchemist*', in R. V. Holdsworth (ed.), *'Every Man in his Humour' and 'The Alchemist': A Casebook*, London: Macmillan, pp. 208–19.

— (1997), *Jonson's Magic Houses*, Oxford: Clarendon.

Duncan, Douglas (1979), *Ben Jonson and the Lucianic Tradition*, Cambridge: Cambridge University Press.

Duncan-Jones, Katherine (2001), *Ungentle Shakespeare: Scenes From His Life*, London: Thomson.

Dutton, Richard (1978), 'The Sources, Text and Readers of Sejanus: "Jonson's integrity in the Story"', *Studies in Philology*, LXXV, 181–98.

— (1996), *Ben Jonson: Authority: Criticism*, London: Macmillan.

Easterling, P. E. (1997), 'Form and Performance', in P. E. Easterling (ed.), *The Cambridge Companion to Greek Tragedy*, Cambridge: Cambridge University Press, pp. 151–77.

Elam, Keir (1980), *The Semiotics of Theatre and Drama*, London: Routledge.

Eliot, T. S. (1951), 'Ben Jonson', in *Selected Essays*, London: Faber & Faber, pp. 147–60.

Ellis, Anthony (2005), 'Senescence in Jonson's *Alchemist*: Magic, Morality and the Debasement of the (Golden) Age', *Ben Jonson Journal*, 12, 23–44.

Escolme, Bridget (2005), *Talking to the Audience: Shakespeare, Performance, Self*, London: Routledge.

Evans, Robert C. (1994), *Jonson and the Contexts of His Time*, London: Associated University Press.

— (1998), '*Sejanus*: Ethics and Politics in the Early Reign of James', in Julie Sanders, Kate Chedgzoy and Susan Wiseman (eds), *Refashioning Ben Jonson*, London: Macmillan, pp. 71–92.

Gibbons, Brian (1968), *Jacobean City Comedy*, London: Rupert Hart-Davis.

Goldhill, Simon (1986), *Reading Greek Tragedy*, Cambridge: Cambridge University Press.

Greene, Thomas M. (1970), 'Ben Jonson and the Centred Self', *Studies in English Literature*, 10, 325–48.

Guibbory, Achsah (1986), *The Map of Time: Seventeenth Century English Literature and Ideas of Pattern in History*, Chicago, IL: University of Illinois Press.

Gurr, Andrew (1992), *The Shakespearean Stage 1574–1642*, 3rd edn, Cambridge: Cambridge University Press.

— (1999), 'Who is Lovewit? What is he?', in Richard Cave, Elizabeth Schafer and Brian Woolland (eds), *Ben Jonson and Theatre*, London: Routledge, pp. 5–19.

— (2004), *Playgoing in Shakespeare's London*, 3rd edn, Cambridge: Cambridge University Press.

Hardman, Christopher (1988), *The Winter's Tale*, Harmondsworth: Penguin.

Haynes, Jonathan (1992), *The Social Relations of Jonson's Theatre*, Cambridge: Cambridge University Press.

Hazlitt, William (1972), *Lectures on the English Comic Writers*; extract in Jonas A. Barish (ed.), *'Volpone': A Casebook*, London: Macmillan, pp. 49–50.

Hinchcliffe, Arnold P. (1985), *Volpone: Text and Performance*, London: Macmillan.

Hirsh, James (1997), 'Cynicism and the Futility of Art in *Volpone*', in James Hirsh (ed.), *New Perspectives on Ben Jonson*, London: Associated University Press, pp. 106–27.

Holdsworth, R. V. (1978), *'Every Man in his Humour' and 'The Alchemist': A Casebook*, London: Macmillan.

— (1980), report in 'Census of Renaissance Drama Productions', *Research Opportunities in Renaissance Drama*, 23, 58–9.

— (1984), report in 'Census of Renaissance Drama Productions', *Research Opportunities in Renaissance Drama*, 27, 130–1.

Howard, Jean E. (1994), *The Stage and Social Struggle in Early Modern England*, London: Routledge.

Hutson, Lorna (1989), 'The Displacement of the Market in Jacobean City Comedy', *London Journal*, 14, 3–16.

Jardine, Lisa (1983), *Still Harping on Daughters: Women and Drama in the Age of Shakespeare*, Hemel Hempstead: Harvester Wheatsheaf.

Jensen, Ejner J. (1985), *Ben Jonson's Comedies on the Modern Stage*, Ann Arbor, MI: UMI Research Press.

Jonson, Ben (1875), *The Works of Ben Jonson, with Notes Critical and Explanatory*, ed. W. Gifford, London: Bickers.

— (1962), *Volpone*, ed. David Cook, London: Methuen.

— (1963), *Bartholomew Fair*, ed. E. M. Waith, New Haven, CT: Yale University Press.

— (1967), *The Alchemist*, ed. F. H. Mares, Manchester: Manchester University Press.

— (1968), *The Alchemist*, ed. S. Musgrove, Edinburgh: Oliver & Boyd.

— (1973), *Catiline*, ed. W. F. Bolton and Jane F. Gardner, London: Edward Arnold.

— (1977), *Bartholomew Fair*, ed. G. R. Hibbard, London: A & C Black.

— (1979), *Epicoene or The Silent Woman*, ed. R. V. Holdsworth, London: A & C Black.

— (1984), *The New Inn*, ed. Michael Hattaway, Manchester: Manchester University Press.

— (1985), *The Oxford Authors: Ben Jonson*, ed. Ian Donaldson, Oxford: Oxford University Press.

— (1986), *Every Man In His Humour*, ed. Simon Trussler, London: Methuen/RSC.

Jonson, Ben (1987), *The Alchemist*, ed. Peter Bement, London: Routledge.
— (1988), *The Staple of News*, ed. Anthony Parr, Manchester: Manchester University Press.
— (1990), *Sejanus: His Fall*, ed. Philip J. Ayers, Manchester: Manchester University Press.
— (1995), *Poetaster*, ed. Tom Cain, Manchester: Manchester University Press.
— (1996), *The Devil is an Ass*, ed. Peter Happé, Manchester: Manchester University Press.
— (1998a), *'Volpone' and Other Plays*, ed. Lorna Hutson, Harmondsworth: Penguin.
— (1998b), *Every Man In His Humour*, ed. Robert N. Watson, London: A & C Black.
— (1999), *Volpone*, ed. Brian Parker and David Bevington, Manchester: Manchester University Press.
— (2000a), *Bartholomew Fair*, ed. Suzanne Gossett, Manchester: Manchester University Press.
— (2000b), *The Magnetic Lady*, ed. Peter Happé, Manchester: Manchester University Press.
— (2003), *Epicoene, or the Silent Woman*, ed. Richard Dutton, Manchester: Manchester University Press.
Kay, W. David (1995), *Ben Jonson: A Literary Life*, London: Macmillan.
Kernan, Alvin B. (1973), 'Alchemy and Acting: The Major Plays of Ben Jonson', *Studies in the Literary Imagination*, 6, 1–22.
Kiernan, Pauline (1996), *Shakespeare's Theory of Drama*, Cambridge: Cambridge University Press.
Knapp, Peggy (1991), 'Ben Jonson and the Publicke Riot', in David Scott Kastan and Peter Stallybrass (eds), *Staging the Renaissance: Reinterpretations of Elizabethan and Jacobean Drama*, London: Routledge, pp. 164–80.
Knights, L. C. (1937), *Drama and Society in the Age of Jonson*, London: Chatto & Windus.
Kuller Shuger, Debora (1990), *Habits of Thought in the English Renaissance: Religion, Politics and the Dominant Culture*, Berkeley, CA: University of California Press.

Kyd, Thomas (1959), *The Spanish Tragedy*, ed. P.W. Edwards, Manchester: Manchester University Press.

Lafkidou Dick, Aliki (1974), *Paideia Through Laughter: Jonson's Aristophanic Appeal to Human Intelligence*, The Hague: Mouton.

Lake, Peter (2002), *The Antichrist's Lewd Hat: Protestants, Papists and Players in Post-Reformation England*, New Haven, CT: Yale University Press.

Leech, Clifford (1973), 'The Incredibility of Jonson's Comedy', in W. Blissett, J. Patrick and R. Van Fossen (eds), *A Celebration of Ben Jonson*, Toronto: Toronto University Press, pp. 3–25.

Leggatt, Alexander (1981), *Ben Jonson: His Vision and his Art*, London: Methuen.

Levin, Richard (1971), *The Multiple Plot in English Renaissance Drama*, Chicago, IL: University of Chicago Press.

Levine, Laura (1994), *Men in Women's Clothing: Anti-theatricality and Effeminization, 1579–1642*, Cambridge: Cambridge University Press.

Loxley, James (2002), *Routledge Guides to Literature: Ben Jonson*, London: Routledge.

Luckyj, Christina (1993), ' "A Moving Rhetoricke": Women's Silences and Renaissance Texts', *Renaissance Drama*, 24, 33–56.

McDermott, Kristen (1993), 'Versions of Femininity in Bartholomew Fair', *Renaissance Papers*, 26, 91–115.

McEvoy, Sean (2004), 'Hieronimo's Old Cloak: Theatrical Representation in Ben Jonson's Middle Comedies', *Ben Jonson Journal*, 11, 67–87.

Mack, Robert L. (1997), 'Ben Jonson's Own "Comedy of Errors": "That Witty Play," *The Case is Altered*', *Ben Jonson Journal*, 4, 47–63.

McPherson, David C. (1974), 'Ben Jonson's Library and Marginalia: An Annotated Catalogue', *Studies in Philology*, LXXI, pp. 43–4.

— (1990), *Shakespeare, Jonson, and the Myth of Venice*, London: Associated University Press.

Marcus, Leah S. (1986), *The Politics of Mirth: Jonson, Herrick, Milton, Marvell and the Defense of Old Holiday Pastimes*, Chicago, IL: University of Chicago Press.

— (1995), 'Of Mire and Authority', in David L. Smith, Richard Strier and David Bevington (eds), *The Theatrical City: Culture,*

Theatre and Politics in London, 1576–1649, Cambridge: Cambridge University Press, pp. 170–81.

Mardock, James (2002), 'Hermaphroditical Authority in Jonson's City Comedies', *Ben Jonson Journal*, 9, 69–86.

Maus, Katherine Eisaman (1984), *Ben Jonson and the Roman Frame of Mind*, Princeton, NJ: Princeton University Press.

Mendes, Sam (1999), 'Sam Mendes talks to Brian Woolland', in R. Cave, E. Schafer and B. Woolland (eds), *Ben Jonson and Theatre*, London: Routledge, pp. 79–85.

Millard, Barbara C. (1984), '"An Acceptable Violence": Sexual Contest in Jonson's *Epicoene*', *Medieval and Renaissance Drama in England*, 1, 143–58.

Miller, Shannon (1996), 'Consuming Mothers/Consuming Merchants: The Carnivalesque Economy of Jacobean City Comedy', *Modern Language Studies*, 26, 73–95.

Mullaney, Steven (1991), 'Civic Rites, City Sites: The Place of the Stage', in D. Scott Kastan and P. Stallybrass (eds), *Staging the Renaissance: Reinterpretations of Elizabethan and Jacobean Drama*, London: Routledge, pp. 17–26.

Mulryan, John (2000), 'Jonson's Classicism', in Richard Harp and Stanley Stewart (eds), *The Cambridge Companion to Ben Jonson*, Cambridge: Cambridge University Press, pp. 163–74.

Newman, Karen (1989), 'City Talk: Women and Commodification in Jonson's *Epicoene*', *Journal of English Literary History*, 56, 503–18.

Noyes, Robert Gayle (1935), *Ben Jonson on the English Stage 1660–1776*, Cambridge, MA: Harvard University Press.

Orgel, Stephen (1996), *Impersonations*, Cambridge: Cambridge University Press.

Ostovich, Helen (1994), 'The Appropriation of Pleasure in *The Magnetic Lady*', *Studies in English Literature*, 34, 425–42.

— (1999a), '"To Behold the Scene Full": Seeing and Judging in *Every Man Out of His Humour*', in Martin Butler (ed.), *Representing Ben Jonson*, London: Macmillan, pp. 76–113.

— (1999b), 'Hell for Lovers: Shades of Adultery in *The Devil is an Ass*', in Martin Butler (ed.), *Representing Ben Jonson*, London: Macmillan, pp. 155–82.

Parker, R. B. (1978), '*Volpone* in Performance: 1921–1972', *Renaissance Drama*, 9, 147–73.

Partridge, Edward (1958), *The Broken Compass*, London: Chatto & Windus.

Petronius (1965), *The Satyricon*, trans. J. P. Sullivan, Harmondsworth: Penguin.

Potter, Lois (1999), 'The Swan Song of the Stage Historian', in Martin Butler (ed.), *Representing Ben Jonson*, London: Macmillan, pp. 193–209.

Rebhorn, Wayne A. (ed.) (2000), *Renaissance Debates on Rhetoric*, Ithaca, NY: Cornell University Press.

Riggs, David (1989), *Ben Jonson: A Life*, Cambridge, MA: Harvard University Press.

Rose, Mary Beth (1988), *The Expense of Spirit: Love and Sexuality in English Renaissance Drama*, Ithaca, NY: Cornell University Press.

Royston, Murray (2003), '*Volpone*: Comedy or Mordant Satire?', *Ben Jonson Journal*, 10, 1–21.

Salmon, J. H. M. (1991), 'Seneca and Tacitus in Jacobean England', in Linda Levy Peck (ed.), *The Mental World of the Jacobean Court*, Cambridge: Cambridge University Press, pp. 169–88.

Sanders, Julie (1998a), *Ben Jonson's Theatrical Republics*, London: Macmillan.

— (1998b), 'Print, Popular Culture and Consumption in *The Staple of News*', in Julie Sanders, Kate Chedgzoy and Susan Wiseman (eds), *Refashioning Ben Jonson*, London: Macmillan, pp. 183–207.

— (2003), '*The New Inn* and *The Magnetic Lady*: Jonson's Dramaturgy in the Caroline Context', in Brian Woolland (ed.), *Jonsonians: Living Traditions*, Aldershot: Ashgate, pp. 51–66.

Schafer, Elizabeth (1999), 'Daughters of Ben', in Richard Cave, Elizabeth Schafer and Brian Woolland (eds), *Ben Jonson and Theatre*, London: Routledge.

Seneca (1966), *Four Tragedies and 'Octavia'*, trans. E. F. Watling, Harmondsworth: Penguin.

Shakespeare, William (1997), *The Riverside Shakespeare*, ed. G. Blakemore Evans and J. J. M. Tobin, Boston: Houghton Mifflin.

Sidney, Sir Philip (1966), *A Defence of Poetry*, ed. J. A. Van Dorsten, Oxford: Oxford University Press.

Smallwood, R. L. (1981) ' "Here, in the Friars": Immediacy and Theatricality in *The Alchemist*', *Review of English Studies*, 23, 142–60.

Sophocles (1984), *The Three Theban Plays*, trans. Robert Fagles, Harmondsworth: Penguin.

Stallybrass, Peter and White, Allon (1986), *The Politics and Poetics of Transgression*, Ithaca, NY: Cornell University Press.

States, Bert O. (1983), 'The Dog on the Stage: Theater as Phenomenon', *New Literary History*, 14, 373–88.

Stone, Lawrence (1965), *The Crisis of the Aristocracy 1558–1641*, Oxford: Oxford University Press.

Swann, Marjorie (1998), 'Refashioning Society in Ben Jonson's *Epicoene*', *Studies in English Literature*, 38, 297–315.

Sweeney, John (1982), '*Volpone* and the Theater of Self-Interest', *English Literary Renaissance*, 12, 220–241.

Tacitus (1989), *The Annals of Imperial Rome*, trans. Michael Grant, Harmondsworth: Penguin.

Teague, Frances (1985), *The Curious History of 'Bartholomew Fair'*, London: Associated University Press.

Watson, Robert N. (1987), *Ben Jonson's Parodic Strategy: Literary Imperialism in the Comedies*, Cambridge, MA: Harvard University Press.

Wayne, Don E. (1982), '*Drama and Society in the Age of Jonson*: An Alternative View', *Renaissance Drama* n.s., 13, 103–29.

— (1999), ' "Pox on Your Distinction!" Humanist Reformation and Deformations of the Everyday in *The Staple of News*', in Patricia Fumerton and Simon Hunt (eds), *Renaissance Culture and the Everyday*, Philadelphia, PA: University of Pennsylvania Press, pp. 67–91.

Weimann, Robert (2000), *Author's Pen and Actor's Voice*, Cambridge: Cambridge University Press.

Wells, Susan (1981), 'Jacobean City Comedy and the Ideology of the City', *English Literary History*, 48, 37–60.

Wheeler, John (1931), *A Treatise of Commerce* (Facsimile), New York: Columbia University Press.

Wickham, Glynne (1981), *Early English Stages 1300–1600, Vol. 3, Plays and their Makers to 1576*, London: Routledge & Kegan Paul.

Womack, Peter (1986), *Ben Jonson*, Oxford: Basil Blackwell.

— (1989), 'The Sign of the Light Heart: Jonson's *The New Inn*, 1629 and 1987', *New Theatre Quarterly*, 5, 162–70.

Woolland, Brian (2002), 'Jonson and British Theatre Since 1900', lecture given at the Society for Theatre Research, Queen Square, London, 18 April 2002; made available by kind permission of the author.

— (2003), 'Sejanus his Fall: Does Arruntius Cry at Night?', in Brian Woolland (ed.), *Jonsonians: Living Traditions*, Aldershot: Ashgate, pp. 27–42.

Young, R. V. (2000), 'Ben Jonson and Learning', in Richard Harp and Stanley Stewart (eds), *The Cambridge Companion to Ben Jonson*, Cambridge: Cambridge University Press, pp. 43–57.

Index